Money Manifestation Mastery

Lara Waldman

*Dear Ilora,
Sending you much
Love & Abundance.
♡ Lara*

Published by New Generation Publishing in 2017

Copyright © Lara Waldman 2017

First Edition

The author asserts the moral right under the Copyright, Designs and Patents Act 1988 to be identified as the author of this work.

All Rights reserved. No part of this publication may be reproduced, stored in a retrieval system or transmitted, in any form or by any means without the prior consent of the author, nor be otherwise circulated in any form of binding or cover other than that which it is published and without a similar condition being imposed on the subsequent purchaser.

www.newgeneration-publishing.com

Acknowledgments

To my husband, Joby, thank you for supporting me with all of my crazy ideas and never standing in the way of my dreams.

To my beautiful children, Kusa and Florence. Thank you for keeping me grounded and reminding me what's truly important in life.

Thank you to all of my clients for helping me birth this work. This information comes through me while supporting you. I wouldn't be here without you.

Deep gratitude to my Soul Sisters, Lysa Black, Karina Ladet, Tara Love Perry and Sarah Stollery, for calling me into more, for loving me while I rise up and for seeing who I truly am. You give me the strength, support and courage to do what I do.

To my flesh and blood Soul sisters Satya and Nicola. It is amazing to be so loved, accepted and understood by you both. I am so blessed to have sisters like you.

To my parents. Thank you for birthing me, for supporting me and for challenging me. I wouldn't be here without you.

I have so many people to share my gratitude for. Thank you to everyone in my life.

For My Daughters

Money Manifestation Mastery
Book Bonus

To support you with your Money Manifestation Mastery Journey, make sure to register for Lara's FREE Book Bonus support.

Visit this link receive your free Money Manifestation Mastery support tools:
http://larawaldman.com/money-manifestation-mastery-book-bonuses/

After you visit this link, follow the instructions to register. You will receive free guided meditations and videos.

Contents

Introduction 1

Chapter 1 20

Chapter 2 41

Chapter 3 65

Chapter 4 103

Chapter 5 152

Chapter 6 184

Chapter 7 230

Chapter 8 237

Conclusion 253

Introduction

'If you want it and expect it, it will be yours very soon.'

– Esther Hicks

Welcome! It is my great honour to share this information with you at this significant point in your life. I trust that this book is in your hands because it is your time to discover this life-changing material. Even if you have done some work with money manifestation before, you are being led to take this practice to the next level and welcome even greater abundance into your life.

If you are waking up to the magic of life, wanting to make a difference in the world, and you are ready to take your finances to the next level, then this book is for you. If you are already doing well financially, but you feel that you are destined for much more, then this book will give you the tools to use your finances to effect profound change for you, your life and the world. We all have ways where we limit ourselves when it comes to money. It's time to lift the lid on what is truly possible for you.

Whatever is going on in your financial life, please know that you are not alone. So many people I speak to feel that they are the only ones who are struggling, they are the only ones who can't figure out how to move through their challenges, essentially feeling like the only ones who have screwed up. Darling one, you are far from screwed up. You are a highly sensitive magical being doing the best that you can at this thing called *life*.

Life is intense. Life can be hard. Life can bring great pain, challenge and struggle… this is part of our human experience on this planet. BUT, I have some good news; it doesn't have to be as hard as you make it. You don't have to stay in the pain, in the struggle, and suffer any longer. There is an easier way.

You see, I know a little secret about you. You have something incredible to share with the world. Your pain, suffering, struggle or inability to move forward is hiding your amazing gifts. Your pain is a sign directing you to your purpose. Are you willing to take the next step to uncover the incredible experiences that life has waiting for you?

I am curious to know what brings you to open this book. Have you been experiencing difficulty in your finances? Have you been experiencing financial lack? Do you have debt? Are you broke? Or do you have money but find you are working too hard for it? Are you feeling dissatisfied and unfulfilled? What is your relationship with money in your life?

You may be getting the call that there is more for you and your life. What is your heart and soul calling out for, dear one? What are you ready for? What do you dream about for your life? If there was a magic wand and you could ask for anything, what would that be? I would like to invite you to dig deep, open your heart and allow yourself to connect to what you truly want from life.

Wherever you are, know that you are in the perfect place. This book has come to you at this time for a reason. I invite you to absorb all of the information here and integrate it into your life. These steps are truly life changing.

In this book, you will be learning my '5 Steps to Abundance Activation'. The five foundational steps to manifesting money and anything else you desire into your life with ease.

These steps are:

Step 1: Relax
Step 2: Release
Step 3: Receive
Step 4: Rhythm
Step 5: Repeat

Although simple and easy to use, these steps are powerful and transformational, but they are not hard! If you only value things in life that are hard, or hard work, it's time to let that go. This process is about welcoming what you want into your life with ease and joy. Would you be willing to receive what you are asking for into your life with greater ease rather than pain and struggle? This is a simple concept but a completely new paradigm of living.

Using the tools in this book will help you to:

a) Get out of your own way and stop pushing money away, and all of the other good things in life.
b) Stop limiting yourself and what is possible for your financial life.
c) Connect deeply to your purpose and the truth of who you are.
d) Show up more powerfully in your life and be here fully while welcoming money into your life.

By the time that you have finished reading this book you will have the tools to manifest money and anything else you desire, with ease, for the rest of your life.

Lara's Money Story

Money had never been a big issue in my life. I hadn't really thought about it much.

I moved to London from Vancouver, Canada, in my early 20s, to attend theatre school. At this point in my life I thought my destiny was to be an actress, and a successful one at that!

I was living at my uncle's house in North London paying very minimal rent while I worked and studied full-time. I had a half-day off a week. I worked very hard over those two years at theatre school, but didn't give much consideration to money matters.

I met my husband in London and about a year later I moved in with him (when he was my boyfriend). Our rent was quite low as we shared a house with friends. I wasn't making a lot of money but I worked full-time and always covered my costs. There wasn't much extra but that didn't bother me. I didn't worry about money or concern myself with it.

I was moving blindly through life, assuming things would just work out. And things did seem to work out. This method of being unconscious around money worked for quite a few years. On reflection, I realise that at this point in my life I had completely turned my back on money. I ignored it. I did not acknowledge its existence.

I grew up in an affluent area in Vancouver, Canada. Enjoying the benefits of wealth was a normal part of our life. Our family, and many of the people around us, skied regularly at the famous ski resort, Whistler. We sailed often on our boat, and took nice holidays in Europe. I didn't realise it at the time, but now I know that we were living a privileged lifestyle and doing very well financially. But I didn't feel this way.

Growing up, I felt that we were tight with money. There was fear attached to any mention of it, and a feeling of lack when it came to the subject of money. The feeling I had as a child was that there wasn't enough and so we had to cling to what we did have.

I observed that the people around us who were seemingly well-off, had no depth to them. Most seemed superficial and spent their time focused on what I judged to be meaningless pursuits. I concluded that rich people were not good people. I didn't want this to become my reality. Unconsciously, I had decided that people with money were greedy, shallow, surface, disconnected, cold and uncaring. Just a few judgements there!

After living in London for a couple of years, my life undertook a radical change. I started meditating after much resistance and awoke to my psychic abilities. In meditation one day I saw in big lights in my mind's eye: 'You are a Healer!' I collapsed on my bed in a flood of tears, as I knew that my acting dreams were no longer going to materialise. It was a big moment in my life when I realised that I was not going to be an actress. I was really pissed off with the Universe!

I had no idea what healing was. I knew it had something to do with helping people by using my hands but that was it. Pissed off, I told the Universe that I would not look for this healing thing; the healing had to come to me. Through a series of serendipitous events, a healing course landed in my lap. After day one on this healing course I knew that healing was my future. Everything flowed very quickly after that point. Very soon I was practicing professionally as a Healer working with clients. It was a period of very rapid growth.

On this healing journey, I had my eyes, heart and soul opened to a completely transformative way of being. This spiritual path I found myself on was my new truth, and seemed to show me the right way to live, as opposed to the unconscious life I had known previously.

I discovered that life was about deep connection with the heart, the soul, and the Universe. I felt as though I had come home, that I had arrived within myself. I felt a sense of peace, love and belonging that I had not felt for a very long time. This experience was something that money could not buy.

This is true, all well and good, but…

At this point in my life I was focused on my passion, helping people heal, to feel better, to thrive, and that's all I wanted. I was practically giving my healing services away, charging very little, because I wanted to help everyone. I was so consumed by what I was doing, and so driven to help others, I didn't even care about money. I got by working part-time in a health food shop and part-time as a Healer, Channel and Spiritual Coach.

When I was 26 years old, I discovered I was pregnant. This was a big surprise! I knew it was the right thing but it was completely unplanned. At this point my husband and I weren't married, which wasn't a problem for a rule breaker like me, but we had never once spoken of our future together. Funnily enough, six months earlier I had said to the Universe, 'If a soul wants to come through me, and it's on my path to being a mother, then I am open and willing.' Perhaps I should have mentioned this to my boyfriend!

Having a baby meant that we would both now be living off my husband's income and we would transition from a shared house with friends, to living with just the three of us together. We lost the income from the lodgers as well as my income.

I was so happy about having a baby that I didn't give money much thought. I was blissfully unaware about finances and was in the space of trusting that it would all work out.

For the most part it did all work out, but over time we began accumulating more and more debt as our spending surpassed our income. My maternity allowance dried up and we continued on this way about nine months until we realised that we had to do something different, as we were deep in overdraft without any additional funds at the end of each month.

I was then gifted $33,000, which was amazing. I am a powerful manifester! But I managed to blow this incredibly quickly. I spent it all on a few items we needed at the time and on our living costs. It got swallowed up in a flash and then I had nothing to show from it. We were back to square one.

To solve our money problems, we decided to add a lodger. This brought in some monthly income and pulled us out of deep waters. Having a someone rent out a room in our home helped but did not solve our financial worries.

At this point my daughter was 18 months old. Our money situation hadn't improved, and our expenses had increased as well as our stress levels. My husband had to bear the brunt of the financial burden, as I was home full-time with our daughter and not earning an income.

That year we got married and on our honeymoon we fell pregnant again. Another surprise! Again, this was a wonderful gift but also came with an increase in financial challenges.

Our situation became more constrained and more stressful. I began to feel more and more stuck, frustrated and limited by our options. I was at home with two young kids, exhausted, with a 'just make it through the day' kind of attitude, without enough money to enjoy even the simple things in life.

What I wanted desperately was sleep! I would have paid thousands for it. But mainly I wanted help with the kids, money to eat out now and then, to be able to give my kids new experiences, to be able to study, to be able to go on nice holidays with the kids, and have a home by the sea. I also knew that I had a meaningful purpose on this planet and being stuck at home, limited in this way, was not part of the bigger picture that I saw for myself.

What was going on here? I was really confused by our situation. This was not what I had seen for my destined life purpose.

Over time I realised that the lifestyle I wanted would require money. And not just a little, but quite a lot, especially if I wanted a house by the sea, and to offer my children wonderful experiences and amazing holidays each year in different, interesting places around the world.

I then bumped up against something very strong within myself that I didn't know existed. I started to feel conflict between what I wanted in regards to my financial reality and what I had unconsciously concluded about money.

I discovered the negative thoughts and beliefs about money I had somehow acquired, such as: 'If you were truly spiritual, you wouldn't want money'. 'Money doesn't buy you happiness'. 'People with money are greedy and shut off from their hearts'. 'People who have lots of money are bad people'. 'Healers who want money or have money are sell-outs', and 'Healers should not charge money, they should give their services away for free'. These are just a few of the ideas that were swimming around my head.

As a result of these inner conflicts about money, I practically gave my services away. At this point I was practicing as a Healer a few hours a week, working my schedule around being at home with my kids. I was attracting clients who were mainly on benefits that really could not afford my services. Even for those that could afford my services, I would find myself offering my discounted rate, even if they didn't ask! I just wanted to help and I didn't care about being compensated, but underneath that there was something deeper going on. I had a very hard time valuing myself and my Healing work when it came to monetary rewards.

As a Healer, I came from the place of wanting to help everyone, and because I love what I do, it never felt like work. My Healing practice wasn't about the money. My goal was about helping people connect with their soul, to find their purpose and to learn to live happily on this planet. But things were not working for us when it came to money.

It wasn't until I got very busy with my practice years later that I took a close look at how I was charging for my work. I was working a lot, scheduling my time around my children's commitments, and I was fully booked, feeling exhausted by all the healing I was doing. Yet, we didn't seem to be that much better off financially.

I decided to write down how much I was earning, how many clients I was working with and how much they were each paying me. No, I had not done this before! My accountant father would be very distressed to hear that. Suddenly, it became very clear to me what was going on. It was an uncomfortable realisation that I was working as many hours as I could as a Healer without having much to show for it. It also dawned on me that I was reaching the limit of how much money I could make. My financial situation was not looking good. I was still not bringing in enough money for us to meet our needs. In addition, I discovered that I was charging most people my discounted rate and therefore it became clear to me that something had to change.

I was in conflict. I was stuck, exhausted and confused. I thought my purpose was to help people through Healing and yet I was challenged by my financial situation. I didn't understand.

I decided to take my dilemma to the higher dimensions and ask for guidance. Thus began the beautiful dialogue between me and the Universe about money, which continued for many years.

Money Message from the Universe

I started to pray and ask for guidance about money. I sat in meditation asking, *'What is Money? Show me what money is all about? What is possible in our relationship with money on this planet? Show me the truth about money.'*

I was shown incredible things psychically about money that completely changed my life. I would like to share these messages with you now, and finally break through the destructive limiting beliefs around money that have been holding you back for far too long.

Guess what?! The Universe wants You to be Wealthy!

When I sat down to receive guidance from the Universe and my inner awareness about money, I was shown an image of a very loving, benevolent being, holding a huge amount money out to me, ready to gift it to me. This being was smiling at me and lovingly said, *'How much are you willing to receive? There is no a limit here, there is just as much as you are willing to let in.'*

I wasn't willing to receive much, it turns out! I was shown how I was energetically blocking the money the Universe had for me from showing up in my life. I was shown the protection and armour I'd built around me that was not allowing this abundance of money love in. I was blocking myself from receiving wealth.

I asked, *'If there is an abundance of money available to me, then why am I blocking it?'* I was then shown that I did not feel worthy enough, good enough or loveable enough to receive it. Digging a little deeper, I could see my belief that it would seem very out of control to receive so much money. It did not feel safe to have an abundance of money. This level of wealth was beyond the world that I knew and was out of my comfort zone. I was stuck in that comfort zone. I was blocking myself from having money, love, support and the joy of living on this planet.

There is no judgement on the other levels of consciousness. You are loved and accepted for whatever you choose. If you choose to block money and stay in lack, the Universe will support you in that and love you through that choice. But equally, if you make a choice to receive more money into your life, you will be helped and supported to receive more money into your life, with love, joy and celebration. You are the creator of your reality. So what do you want to choose?

You do not have to struggle! We make this life much, much harder than it needs to be. Receiving money in alignment with your soul's purpose is to allow yourself the experience of joy, love and abundance. It is your true nature to experience joy, love and abundance, as your true nature *is* joy, love and abundance. Receiving money is therefore in alignment with your true nature.

Being financially abundant allows you to experience all of the wonderful things that life has to offer you. Receiving money is another way that you can receive love, support and the best of all that is available in life. This is what I call the 'Joy of Living'.

One of my first big dreams was to gift my husband the gift that he had given me. My husband, Joby, has always fully supported me in following my heart and my dreams. After having kids, I've never had to take a day job just to pay the bills. I have worked as a Healer, Channel and a Spiritual Coach, as well as being able to stay home with my kids, which was really important to us both at the time.

That first dream was to bring my business to a level that would allow my husband to be able to follow his heart and no longer have to work just to support the family.

This dream of growing my business took me on a journey of healing my relationship with money and learning how to love and value myself. As a result, by shifting my relationship with money and taking guided action to grow my business, my business has grown dynamically, which allowed my husband to hand in his notice in January 2016 at a job he had held for 16 years.

Joby felt huge pressure to provide for the family, and now as a result of the changes that I made in both myself and my career, he was able to follow his heart and start up his own business. This was the first dream that we have made a reality. There were many more exciting dreams to come, but this was a milestone for us.

What would be an exciting milestone for you to reach?

This is what I learned from the Universe about money:

- Money is just energy, it's not good or bad.
- Money is life-force energy, Universal energy, creative energy, whose natural state is flow and abundance.
- It is your natural state to be in flow with money,

receiving it into your life in abundance.
- There is an infinite supply of money available to you.
- You can make a greater impact in the world with money than without money; staying limited financially serves no one.
- The effect of money is determined by each individual and how they choose to use it, rather than 'money being the root of all evil', as some like to say. Money is just an amplifier of what is going on internally within each individual.
- The Universe wants to gift you as much money as you are willing to receive.
- Your true nature is that of abundance. Financial abundance is a deeper expression of your true nature than lack and poverty. Abundance is being in the flow with the Universe, your true nature, your soul or higher self.
- Welcoming in wealth and abundance is the expression of Universal love, joy, freedom and possibility.
- Money is connected to your relationship with your purpose, your true self (higher self, soul), self-love, self-worth, your power and your sexuality.

Welcoming money into your life is a choice. It is not good or bad to have money but you are very welcome to say *yes* to money.

This journey to money manifestation mastery goes so much deeper than just acquiring more money. This is a journey into you, uncovering the truth of who you are, revealing your purpose and why you are here on this earth at this time. Your money manifestation is a journey to greater joy, freedom, empowerment, and the pleasure of being alive! Money manifestation is the vehicle to revealing the greatest truth about who you truly are, your magic, your gifts and your power. We are about to take an exciting adventure together.

In this book you will discover how to become a 'Money Manifestation Master'. You will be learning my 5 steps to 'Abundance Activation', how to manifest more wealth into your life in alignment with your soul's purpose. This is about manifesting money and anything else that your heart and soul desires, with flow, ease, joy and fulfilment. I hope you are ready to break through the old money paradigms and start experiencing a life of greater joy, peace, freedom and financial abundance.

This is a process of empowerment and of deep self-discovery. As you move through these steps you are going to uncover the hidden jewels and gems that you have been hiding away from yourself and the world. 'Money Manifestation Mastery' is a life-changing process.

'Financial Freedom' is about your power and the expression of your purpose. When you are in financial lack or scarcity, this keeps you in survival mode. Living in survival mode limits your impact in the world. My wish for you is that you have all the money that you need so that you can stop worrying about having enough and get on with your greater purpose in the world. Imagine what you would do if all of your financial needs were met? If you had all the resources that you could ever need, what would you choose to do with your life?

It's time to move from living in disempowerment, lack and scarcity so you can make the impact that you were born to make and experience the full magic of life that is possible for you.

This book is designed to help you manifest money into your life on the energetic level. Your emotions, mindset, thoughts and beliefs need to be balanced and aligned in order to manifest finances into your life. This book will teach you all about the inner game of money manifestation. Get ready to take your connection with yourself, your purpose and the Universe to the next level.

Chapter 1

What is Abundance Activation?

'Abundance Activation' is the practice of unlocking what is truly possible for you and your life here on this planet by connecting you with your true essence, which is abundance. We are speaking specifically about 'Financial Abundance', an abundance of wealth, an abundance of money flowing into your life with ease and joy. We are talking about money, honey! But the principles you will be learning apply to manifesting an abundance of anything that your heart and soul desires into your life.

Your true nature is that of abundance, flow, joy and limitless possibilities. Your true self also includes an abundance of money, if you so choose. 'Abundance Activation' is about clearing the ways that you block money, and all other good things in life, from flowing into your life, and welcoming in the abundant flow just waiting to pour in.

An added bonus of money manifestation is that when you focus on welcoming more riches into your life, that ability can improve other areas of your life as well. The practice of 'Abundance Activation' will enhance your relationships, your health, and your work, as well as your feelings of happiness and fulfillment.

You are in flow with your abundance when you are connected to your true being, also known as your higher self or the soul. With this flow of abundance you are connecting to all that is possible for you and your life by connecting to who you truly are.

Although this flow of abundance is your true state of being, there are blocks and barriers that you have unconsciously created to this Universal flow. By activating your abundance you are releasing your money blocks, the barriers, and the obstacles to this divine flow so you can come back to your truth and unlock your financial floodgates.

'Abundance Activation' is about realising your purpose, what you are here to do, what you are here to experience and be in your life on this planet. The deeper impact of activating your abundance is that you will show up more powerfully in your life, being fully here on this planet, embodying your purpose.

Being in your abundant flow has a huge impact on all life around you, on the planet, and on humanity. Being in tune with your abundance feels good! When you activate your abundance, you are in harmony with your true self, you are fully present and acting in accordance with your purpose. This allows you to feel happy, peaceful, joyful, clear, connected to the Universe and those around you, and supported by them. There is a feeling of greater fulfillment, ease and ability in your life from this place of abundance.

Money is a Vehicle

The process of 'Abundance Activation' involves more than money alone. I see money as a vehicle to help you strengthen your purpose in life, to become who you are designed to be and inviting you to show up more powerfully in your life. The process of money manifestation helps you to love, value and honour yourself. As you do, this sends transformational ripples of change out into the world, which gives others permission to do the same. The deeper purpose of this 'Abundance Activation' process is for you to recognise your truth, and in so doing, to go out into the world and be the change that you were born to make.

When you activate your abundance, not only do you get the benefit of having more money and everything that money brings, but you will also actualise the truth of who you are, and this is why I am writing this book; it's the more profound purpose of these money manifestation tools that gets me excited for you and your journey.

Why is it Important to Activate your Abundance?

The process of activating your financial abundance and welcoming more money into your life runs much deeper than actual money. How money shows up in your life is the cursory expression of something more profound happening within you and your relationship with life. To welcome more money into your life requires you to do some inner work and soul searching.

What is it that is blocking you from welcoming in financial riches? With that simple question, we can uncover old emotional baggage that is part of the great dam blocking the river of money that is waiting to flow to you.

Welcoming in financial abundance requires you to examine your limiting thoughts, beliefs, emotions, family programming, ancestral programming, cultural programming and societal programming that is stopping you from receiving wealth into your life with ease. What lies in the way of you having a wonderful experience with money?

Money manifestation is about your relationship with yourself, your relationship with life and the Universe, your relationship with your purpose and your place upon this earth. As you give your love and attention to money, you are giving your love and attention to all of these other aspects of life as well, starting with you.

Everything that I am going to be sharing with you is ultimately about learning to love and value yourself. When you love and value yourself, when you honour yourself fully, and your place upon this Earth, you move into your natural abundance. As you give your focus and attention to manifesting more money, you are giving your focus and attention to yourself at the same time. As you learn to give money the love and attention it needs to grow, you will experience incredible growth and expansion personally at the same time.

Your money blocks, your limiting thoughts, beliefs and programming around money, are designed to keep you small, limited and in hiding. These money blocks are stopping you from living your life to the fullest. Welcoming more financial rewards into your life helps you to live life to your full potential while strengthening your sense of self and your self-worth.

Money manifestation helps you to show up more powerfully in your life, realise your purpose and to make a greater impact in the world. Staying small, limited, in lack and disempowered serves no one, including you.

Ripples of Transformation

Showing up more fully in your life makes a powerful difference on this planet. Your inner work has a positive, transformational rippling effect. This is exactly what the world needs. As you focus within, you shift without. Your personal change sends ripples of positive change out into the world. It's time to end the pain and suffering on this planet, starting with you.

The deeper purpose of this book, and why I am sharing these money manifestation tools with you, is that I know you are needed here. There are parts of you that are still in hiding; there are parts of you that are afraid to step into your destiny, and there are parts of your genius and your gifts that you are keeping a secret. The world needs you, but more importantly, 'you need you'.

Welcoming more money into your life is about your coming out of the shadows, shining your light, empowering yourself and others as well as living a life of fun, joy and possibility.

When you are moving through life from a place of financial lack or working way too hard for money, you are cut off and distracted from the full expression of your *being* and what is possible for your life. In these next chapters, you will be learning dynamic but simple techniques to help you manifest money in a way that creates abundance in all areas of your life. It's time to unlock the money manifestation magic!

Creating a New Paradigm with Money

A lot of the heart-centred 'Helpers and Healers' that I speak to have a hard time when it comes to welcoming more money into their life because they have seen many examples of the 'dark side' of money.

With the acquisition of money, we have seen the abuse of power, corruption, destruction, greed, harm to others and the planet. It's painful to observe. From this perspective, many people have concluded that money is 'the root of all evil', the cause of these negative results.

Money is as an amplifier. It's not money that is the root of all evil; money amplifies what is present within each individual or entity and that inner reality is expressed in how they use wealth in the world. Money can amplify the shadow side of a person or business; it can bring out all sorts of unpleasant traits, but only those energies that already exist. Money doesn't make a person 'bad'. It is simply a reflection of the character of an individual as seen in how they use finances in their life and in the world.

Money is similar to sex. You can have a terrible,

hurtful, painful sexual experience but you can also have an amazing, pleasurable, transcendent sexual experience. A hurtful sexual experience doesn't make all sex bad. There are many varied experiences that one can have when it comes to sex. The type of sexual experience depends on the individuals having sex. Money is the same. You can have an experience of money that hurts, corrupts, destructs or harms, but equally money can be empowering, supportive, life-changing and transformational. Money is not good or bad; it's the person or entity with the money and how they use it that determines the positive or negative effect.

So many people are cut off from their truth. Their pain, their feelings of separation, create actions that hurt themselves and others. It's essential that we reconnect to our hearts, our true nature, and our true selves in order to create a new reality on this planet.

You can't change anyone else. You can only change yourself. As you transform within, you can inspire others to do the same but you can't force anyone to do the same. Trust me, I have tried! It doesn't work. The more that each individual shifts their inner world, reconnects to their heart and truth, the greater impact this will have in the world.

We are looking at creating a new paradigm with money; an experience of money that creates joy, freedom and empowerment of the individual and the collective. Here we are examining how to have a new relationship with money, one where you are empowered and you can also empower others.

What do you want from your relationship with money? How do you want to use money in this world? Make a choice to enrich yourself and others, to help yourself and others. To experience a life of joy, expansion and freedom. It's up to you. It's in your hands.

Money in itself may not make you happy, but how about the possibility of being happy, fulfilled, and having all you that desire. How about the possibility of doing work you love, in a way that works for you? It doesn't need to be either/or. You can ask for both: happiness, joy, fulfillment, *and* money. Yes, you can!

Permission to be Wealthy

Before we go any further, we need to start with something really important. The Universe and I are here to give you permission to be wealthy. You have permission to say yes to a life of great riches *and* happiness! Not only do you have permission to be wealthy, but you could argue that it is your duty upon this earth.

I would like to ask you a question. Feel into the answer

on an intuitive level.

'How can you make a bigger impact in the world? With money or without money?'

Think about that for a minute. What comes to you? Every person I have asked always says: *'We can make a greater impact in the world with money.'* Can you help more people and make this world better with money?

Of course, you can still make an impact without money but staying broke, poor or limited financially is not serving anyone, especially not you. You have permission to be wealthy; you have permission to say yes to money; you have permission to be powerful, to have a wonderful life, to thrive and to be happy. Not only because this is awesome for you, but because in allowing this to be your reality, you will make a more positive impact on all life around you.

It's not good or bad to have money, it's simply a choice. What choice will create the greatest result for your life and the lives of others? What comes to your awareness with that question?

Your Money Commitment

Please read through the following statement and sign if you are ready to commit.

'I commit to saying YES to money each and every day. I commit to moving through anything and everything that is holding me back from welcoming more money into my life with ease and joy. I commit to welcoming wealth into my life in alignment with my true authentic self.'

Signed _____

Growing Your Money Garden

Money needs your attention to grow, much like a garden does. In order for a garden to grow, in order to grow fruits and vegetables, you need to give your love, attention and care to that garden regularly, sometimes every day, for it to give back to you with delicious fresh food to eat. It's very similar with money.

Wanting more money without giving money the attention it needs to grow is like asking for an amazing relationship without giving your partner the love and care they need. Can you imagine having a partner that you ignore, neglect and say unkind things to? Can you imagine a relationship where you put the other person down all the time, judging them harshly? How nurturing is that relationship going to be?

It's very clear when you look at the garden analogy or

the relationship analogy what is required for them to thrive, and yet many people don't think about this when it comes to money. Money is something that needs your love, care and attention.

The Universe wants to gift to you, and money wants to flow into your life. Money wants to expand, explore and play in your life. But money also needs a space to be; it needs your love and care in order to yield the results you want.

It's all about choice. You can choose to kill a garden through neglect or lack of care. You can kill a human relationship through neglect and lack of care. The garden is designed to grow and thrive, and that's exactly what money wants to do. What do you choose? Are you ready to start taking care of your financial responsibilities?

Money Journal

To help you get the most from your 'Money Manifestation' journey, buy yourself a special journal dedicated to your money journey. Gift yourself with a journal that you love holding and seeing. In this journal, you will write everything that comes up for you around money over the course of this book and in your 'Abundance Activation' journey beyond.

In this journal you can write down everything regarding your relationship with money. Use your journal as a space to record all the negative, limiting thoughts and beliefs you have around money. Use your journal to share your insights about money. Once you start paying attention, you will notice that these thoughts come up regularly, sometimes every day, throughout the day. Take five minutes each day to journal about your relationship with money.

The first step to releasing your money blocks is awareness. The more aware you are of where you are blocking yourself with your thoughts and beliefs, the easier it will be to unblock these strongholds.

Your Money Manifestation Intention

You are now going to focus on what you want. You need to be clear on what you are asking for before you can manifest your dreams into your reality.

What amount of money, each month, or each year, would give you financial freedom? What is that for you? Every person is unique. Financial freedom for you will be different for others. Financial freedom is also a feeling. What amount of money would give you the feeling of freedom?

WOW Goal

Start with your big WOW goal. This is the dream amount you would like to receive. What would be an awesome sum of money to bring in each month or each year?

Write this number below or in your journal.

£100,000 per annum

First-Step Goal

Once you have your WOW amount of money, please write down your first-step goal. This would be an increase to what you are bringing in now that would give you the feeling that matters are progressing financially for you in your life. It's the money you would feel really good about receiving either each month or each year as a first-step goal. What is that amount for you? Write this amount below or in your journal.

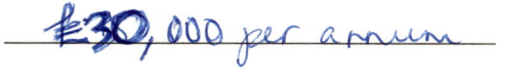

£30,000 per annum

Having a first-step goal can help your mind grasp that change is possible. When a goal is too big it can sometimes seem out of reach. This can cause your limiting self to unconsciously sabotage any progress you may have made. That first-step goal can help you start to take action with smaller baby steps.

Your Money Manifestation Fuel

Why is this amount of money important to you? This money will bring you an experience or a feeling. The feeling behind the money that you are asking for is the true motivation for having more financial abundance in your life.

Your money WHY has to be strong and meaningful for you. Your money WHY will be what fuels you to bring about the changes necessary to make this dream happen. This will be what moves you from your comfort zone into the unknown. There will be moments on your money manifestation journey when it will feel too scary to change your life; these are the moments when you will need to revisit your WHY to find motivation and keep moving forward.

Journal now on why this money is important to you. Hint: it usually comes down to a feeling that you want to experience i.e. freedom, joy, peace, or any other positive emotion.

Keep your money WHY close to your heart. Sometimes this money manifestation journey can get uncomfortable and there will be a strong pull to stop, or reverse the progress you've made. Your money WHY will give you strength to keep going, even when you come up against your biggest obstacles.

Answer the following questions:

Why is this amount of money important to you?
What is the impact of having this money in your life?
Write down the first answers that come to you.
Now look at the answers that you just wrote and ask:
What would be the impact of this in your life?
What would this do?
Why is this important to you?
This next question is a powerful question to ask yourself. Close your eyes and feel into this question.
How much are you willing to receive?
Take this question into meditation, close your eyes and feel into the answer. How much are you willing to receive? You can block yourself from receiving money with ease and joy without even realising it.
What is blocking you from receiving more?
Write the answers that come up for you with that question in your journal.

How to get the Most out of this Book

Momentum is the key to your success. You need to keep feeding your energy into money growth. Your focus is so powerful. Your attention on transforming your relationship with money for the better is what will create positive financial change in your life. Where your attention goes, energy flows.

Take responsibility for yourself and your results—you are the creator of your life. Your financial future is in your hands. No more playing the victim, no more blaming, no more giving your power away to your past. What future are you going to create? The choice is yours.

Give daily consideration to your relationship with money. Spend time in the evening reflecting on anything that came up about money in the day. There's so much that goes on unconsciously all the time. The trick is to watch what appears for you, catching it, and taking notice of it so that you clear everything that is blocking you from manifesting your dreams into reality.

Practice and integrate the '5 Steps to Abundance Activation' daily as you learn these steps in this book.

Commit fully to your self-growth and self-development.

What you need to succeed:

- Get Support.
- Find an accountability buddy, someone to take this journey with you.
- Be kind to yourself.
- Trust there is a process.
- Maintain patience.
- Develop perseverance—a do-whatever-it-takes attitude!
- Be willing to fully show up in your life.

I would now like to share with you the '5 steps to Abundance Activation' to help you manifest more money into your life and improve your relationship with money, which ultimately leads you to experiencing greater joy, freedom and abundance in every area of life.

Please note that this is not a quick-fix solution. These '5 steps to Abundance Activation' are a practice I recommend you do on a daily basis in order to experience the greatest results. I still follow these steps every day. Financial freedom is a journey that requires time, trust and perseverance. I don't believe there is an end to this journey of expansion. So please remember to enjoy the ride.

Vision Board

A 'Money Manifestation Vision Board' is a powerful tool

to keep you on track with your intentions and dreams. A vision board is a place where you can see your dreams, your intentions, and your goals every day. The vision board is designed to remind you of what you are asking for, where you are going, where you are heading, every day.

It's easy to get caught up in negativity, drama and old patterns. You can be easily pulled off the path of your vision. Your vision board is there to remind you of what you want to create moving forward in your life.

I want to keep this as simple as possible so you can take action quickly and easily. I recommend getting a pin board, post-it notes, and push pins. Simply write down each of your intentions on a separate post-it note and put them all on your vision board. You can start by writing the amount of money you are asking for and your money WHY in words detailing what you want. If you are a more creative, visual person, you can draw pictures of what you want or you can cut out photos from magazines depicting what you want. Make your vision board as beautiful as you like. Start simple and then expand your vision board over time.

Buy a pin board, pins and post-it notes. On your vision board write down…

- Yur first-step money goal.
- Your Wow goal.
- Your money WHY.

I would also like you to pin on your vision board the new healthy money mindsets you are intending to adopt. For example, if you have been struggling with self-worth, not feeling good enough, what is the alternative mindset you would like to have? Self-love! You can write in words on your board, 'Self-love', or 'I Love myself', or 'I value myself'. Transform all of your negative money mindsets into positive ones and write those affirmations on your vision board. This is a good way to remind yourself of where you are going and what you will achieve.

On your vision board include the physical objects or experiences you would like as well, and the items or events your money goal will provide for you.

End of Chapter Actions

- Sign up to Lara's Bonus materials to support you with this book: http://larawaldman.com/money-manifestation-mastery-book-bonuses/
- How much money would bring you financial freedom? Each month or year?

- Why is this important to you? What is the impact of this amount of money? Write down the answers. Ask the three questions again for the second set of answers. This process takes you deeper and deeper into your WHY.
- Money Journal: buy yourself a beautiful journal that you dedicate to your money journey. Write in your money journal every day sharing everything that comes up for you about money as you go through this workbook.
- Have a daily check-in on money: in your money journal, write anything that you observe about your relationship with money. Reflect on your relationship with finances every day. What are your thoughts, feelings and emotions that appeared around money today?
- How much are you willing to receive? Write down the answer.
- How do you feel about money? What does money mean to you? What does money do? Journal on these questions.
- Buy yourself a vision board: put your Wow goal and your money WHY on your vision board.
- Journal on *If I had $100,000,000 what would I choose?* How can you bring more of that into your life now?

Chapter 2

Step 1: Relax

'Doing is never enough if you neglect being.'
– Eckhart Tolle

How do you like the idea of making more money while doing less? Well, I have some great news for you, doing nothing is my Number 1 first step to manifesting more money into your life. What?! It's true! Doing nothing is my first step, my secret sauce ingredient to creating your ideal life and your ideal financial reality from a place of ease and joy.

As a society, we have been trained to do, do, doody do. In our world, being super busy is considered a sign of being successful. Keep going, don't stop, don't feel. And if you do stop, distract yourself somehow with eating, drinking or watching TV. Even better, do all three at once. The core message here is that you have to work hard, be stressed and busy in order to make money.

We have been taught that if you do more you will get more done. So we get busier and busier and busier trying to keep on top of the spiraling-out-of-control events of our lives. This leads to high levels of stress, anxiety, feeling overwhelmed and ultimately burned out.

This way of being takes you out of your natural flow. Being super busy stops you from connecting deeply with yourself, with your life and with the Universe. When you are out of sync with yourself and the Universe, you block that natural connection, which leads you to blocking your abundance.

Yes, you can be successful and make a lot of money from this busy, doing energy, but it comes at a great cost. I would like to teach you how to experience abundance in a way that is sustainable and is in harmony with the way you and your body are meant to live.

Female bodies are not designed to work in the same manner that male bodies do. Successful women have been modelling the masculine lifestyle and methods of conducting business and this has been taking its toll. This way of being has proved destructive to both men and women. With the '5 Steps to Abundance Activation', I will be teaching you the feminine way of creating your life and making money. This is much more in keeping with how your true nature is meant to operate.

When I speak about the feminine way of creating your life, I am referring to the energy of the divine feminine. There is also the divine masculine energy. The divine masculine and feminine energies are not about men and women specifically; rather, they are energies within both men and women. The divine masculine and feminine is the same as Yin and Yang. The feminine, Yin, energy is expansive, still, passive, surrendered, open and receiving. The masculine, Yang, energy is about action, direction and focus. You need both sides to achieve balance.

Our society has been run by an out-of-balance masculine and feminine energy in our more recent history. Any energy out of tune with its purpose can become unhealthy and destructive. It's time to come back to our original design and rediscover the gifts of the divine feminine and masculine energies in balance and harmony.

The '5 Steps to Abundance Activation' address this energetic imbalance and lead to an inner unification of your divine nature.

To restore these energies we are going to take a close look at reigniting the gifts of the divine feminine energy within you and your life.

Step 1: Relax. This is the practice of taking time out from your busy schedule to sit and be present with yourself every day. We live in such a hectic time; there are so many demands on your time, attention and energy. There is so much information, the noise of the world, coming at you each day. Relaxing gives you a chance to let your mind, body and spirit rebalance. This must be your number one priority to effect positive change in your life.

Most people think they will relax once they have accomplished every task. My experience is that doing the exact opposite, putting 'Step 1: Relax' first, brings the greatest result. It's counterintuitive to relax before doing, it feels all wrong, but let me show you why this is essential if you are going to manifest your financially abundant life.

Taking time out each day for relaxation allows you to have greater balance, clarity and peace of mind. From this clear place within, you can continue forward in your day with greater ease. The most surprising result of all is that you become more productive and effective this way. You get things done faster and easier, without all the anxiety and stress.

Most of the stuff in your life that stresses you out is simply the noise in your head from emotional and mental imbalance. All the distress you experience makes everything seem far worse than it actually is. Stress, anxiety and feeling overwhelmed will make mountains out of the molehills of everyday occurrences. These negative emotions take you off track and make life so much harder than it needs to be.

When you relax, you give your mind, body, thoughts and emotions a chance to move back into their natural balance. This will give you greater perspective, clarity and peace of mind. When you are working from this place of harmony, you know exactly what you need to do and you do it much more quickly and efficiently. From this place of rest, what you do doesn't feel like hard work. Everything flows with ease from this place of balance.

Make time and space to stop and relax each day. Make this practice a top priority. If you are new to this, I recommend fitting time in for 'Step 1: Relax' at the start of your day, before you get swept up in the energy of daily events. Once you get on that busy train, it can be difficult to get off. Pencil this time in your diary every day. Make this your #1 priority, not your last. The discipline of purposefully relaxing won't happen unless you decide to make it an important part of your day.

With repetition and experience you will hopefully begin to understand why taking time out to relax is so vital. This is not just a luxury, although it is luxurious! This is an essential practice for creating your financially free life.

When you are more balanced mentally and emotionally you experience greater clarity, peace and connection. This connection is the key to abundance. All of the others steps to 'Abundance Activation' stem from this first step, so don't leave it out!

This first step may seem simple but it's profound and

life changing. Give yourself space and time to integrate this step into your life because 'Step 1: Relax' is the foundation of 'Money Manifestation Mastery'. This is the first step to learning 'how to manifest money in the feminine way'. This is money manifestation with ease and joy rather than through hard work and forced action.

How good would it feel…?

- To have time just for you each day.
- To stop and do nothing.
- To feel relaxed.
- To let go.
- To feel peaceful.
- To feel balanced.
- To feel in flow with your life.

What if relaxing was the most defining and primary way to welcome more money into your life? Would you make time and space for it? Would you make it a priority? If you already have a regular meditation practice, that's brilliant, let this be a reminder of its importance. If you don't have a practice for relaxing each day, I want to encourage you to begin one because it is a powerful foundational step, not only to 'Money Manifestation', but also for every area in your life.

With this first step, you are *getting out of your own way.*

The Universe Wants to gift to you. In fact, it's your true nature to receive from the Universe all the time. But *unconsciously you block* this for all sorts of reasons. When you are rushing around, distracted and disconnected, you also block abundance. When you stop to relax, you are undoing all the ways that you stop the flow of receiving. You want to stop the frenetic pace and undo all of the noise, busyness and distraction, in order to get into this natural state of accepting what the Universe wants to gift you. Slow down to consciously start tapping into this energy. When you take time to be still, you become attuned to your natural rich supply.

When you relax, it's like pressing reset on your mind, thoughts and emotions. You are wiping clean your inner slate. When you slow down and clear the mind, you get on track and in agreement with your intentions. Your busy thoughts take you off-track from how you are designed to function, so it's important to slow the mind every day so you don't go too far off course and return to the path you have chosen.

In this space you receive intuition, inner guidance, insight and wisdom about the next step and how to move forward towards financial freedom.

What will it take to welcome this money into your life? The answers exist already. Many of the answers exist within you. You have the ability to tap into infinite wisdom, infinite information from the Universe, from your higher-self, but you need to calm your mind and body enough to receive it, to hear it and to tap into this information.

This connection and wisdom is always there within you, it has never left you, however, when you are constantly doing, with a busy mind, it's hard to hear that inner guidance.

There is so much distraction and sound in the world that blocks you from hearing and feeling on a more meaningful level. Slow down, clear the noise in your mind, and you can receive the intuitive direction that will guide you forward.

From this place of greater clarity and stillness, you are working in a completely new paradigm. The old paradigm you have been trained in is the 'work hard' mentality: 'work hard for everything you get', 'work hard for reward', and 'work hard to manifest money'. This creates crippling stress and tension in your mind and body. You can make money from this place, but at what cost?

The truth is that you don't have to 'work hard' for money, and I want to help you to reprogramme your thoughts by reading this book. The energy that comes from strenuous labour will shut off your natural flow.

This first step 'Relax', does not mean that you don't work. You will still take action, perhaps a lot of action, but not from the energy of hard work. All action that you take is ideally moving forward from the energy of rest. Now, you will move in and out of that space, maybe every day, throughout the day, but remember to come back to that place of connection and flow every time you get off track.

This is not about being perfect, it's about catching yourself when you fall into that hard work mentality or when life is getting stressful. You need to recognise those moments and say: 'I am out of the flow. All right, stop, relax, reset.' Continuing forward from a place of restoration feels so much better.

How do you know when you are out of the current of abundance?

Any heaviness, negative emotions, mental noise and stress you experience is the energetic junk that pulls you out of abundance. If you are feeling down, with low energy, feeling negative or stressed, you have moved out of the flow. This is a sign that something within needs attention.

Staying in the influx of abundance is a practice. It's not about perfection. It's completely human, natural and normal to go through challenging times. What you want to do is actively bring yourself back every time you notice yourself out of the flow. This may even be a moment-to-moment practice at times.

Lara's Story

My family was very busy when I was growing up. I was the kind of child that would have three after-school sporting activities in one day. We were very active as a family and there was not much down-time spent relaxing in my childhood.

When I was in my early 20s I was working full-time, studying full-time and exercising five days a week. My life was go, go, go. What a crazy time! When I exercised I would push myself hard. In fact, I pushed myself hard with everything I did. I was a perfectionist, or at least trying to be perfect. Although it was exhausting, I got a big buzz out of living this way. But this way of being came at a cost.

A few years later I began to get ill every time I exercised. I would then slow down until I got better, and when I was well, I started to exercise again. Soon I would get ill after exercising just one time. This went on for a while until I finally got the message. My body was forcing me to stop and slow down. This is often what illness does, it forces you to hear what is truly going on within.

Needless to say, I was very frustrated by this. I used exercise to channel my pain, discomfort and emotions, so stopping was difficult for me. But it also came with an important message that I was ignoring.

At this point my body could only tolerate very gentle exercise such as yoga and swimming. I was so annoyed and agitated by this but I didn't have much of a choice. Around the same time, I started my meditation practice, which I also found really difficult and uncomfortable, but over time I finally acknowledged its value.

Over time it became clear to me what was going on. I was being forced to connect to a deeper part of myself. Through this experience, I developed a more meaningful relationship with myself, the Universe and my purpose. When I no longer occupied myself with constant activity, I became aware of the subtle information that was trying to reach me and guide me forward on my path.

Staying in motion is a very effective way to avoid feeling. Most people stay busy, busy, busy, so they don't have to recognise the truth of what is going on within and around them. This can take the form of avoiding current life circumstances or pain from your past. Most people have not been taught the tools they need to deal with their feelings. We have been taught to shut down and keep soldiering on.

Because of these deeper emotions affecting you unconsciously, you may have a strong resistance to making time to sit and be with yourself. If there is resistance to 'Step 1: Relax', it will most likely be unconscious. Let me highlight how it may show up for you. This resistance will most likely show up in the form of…

1) I don't have time, I am way too busy.
2) Forget about making time to stop and relax.
3) I will get around to it next week, next month, on holiday, next lifetime.

Please know that if you are not taking time to relax, resistance is in operation. Don't mistake it for something else. See it for what it is.

Meditation

My top practice for 'Step 1: Relax' is meditation. When you think of relaxing you may think of watching TV or having a glass of wine. That's all well and good but it won't get you the results I am speaking about here. What you want to create is a conscious space to relax in, one that is going to activate your abundance.

I recommend meditating for a minimum of 20 minutes each day. If you can't do 20 minutes, how much time can you commit to each day? Five minutes is better than no minutes.

Meditation is the practice of simply being with yourself, present in the moment. If you don't already do so, here is how you meditate:

Step 1) Commit to a certain time each day when you will sit for a minimum of 20 minutes. I personally recommend doing this in the morning, as it's much easier to wake up 20 minutes early than to try to fit it in at another point in the day. Committing to the same time each day helps to create this new, healthy habit. I recommend 20 minutes because it can often take this long before your mind starts to slow down.

Step 2) Switch off all distractions, such as your phone or computer. If you are meditating in the morning, do this before you switch on your phone or computer. It's too easy to become sidetracked while you are meditating. Help yourself stay focused by limiting your distractions.

Step 3) Get comfortable. Sit up in a way that you find relaxing, with your feet flat on the floor or your legs crossed. Add a support for your back if that is more comfortable. It's ideal to have good posture while meditating to assist the flow of energy through your body, but only if this feels comfortable. Don't force yourself into any position that creates tension.

Step 4) Breathe. Simply observe as you inhale and exhale. Your mind will wander. When you notice your mind wandering, come back to your breath. Be present with what you feel physically and emotionally. Observe your experiences without judgement.

Step 5) Let it be and don't have an agenda. If your mind slows and is still, that's great, but don't make that your goal. If your mind is busy, that's fine. Just observe where you are in the moment without judgement. Eventually, your mind will settle if you sit long enough, bringing you into greater balance, peace and clarity.

Your mind needs time and space to process all the information that you are exposed to each day. Information that comes from the television, radio, social media, advertising, phone calls, emails, friends, family, interactions on the street, in the shop, on the bus, driving in your car… all needs time to be processed. You are constantly being inundated with facts and figures. You need approximately 20 minutes to filter all of this information every day, especially if you live in an urban environment. Your mind may be whirling as it processes. With time, your mind will begin to settle. Be patient.

If you have a lot going on emotionally, personally, at work or with your family, your mind may become extra busy. You may need longer to achieve stillness during these times. Personally, I find that if I have an emotional challenge or trigger, I may need to sit for 30 to 40 minutes as I process these thoughts before my mind relaxes. Give yourself the time and space to work through them and you will find that peace comes eventually.

When you are in a place of balance, you naturally move into flow with yourself and the Universe, which is the first step to 'Abundance Activation'.

If you want help with meditation, I have a free guided meditations to support you which you can access in the book bonus page link here:

http://larawaldman.com/money-manifestation-mastery-book-bonuses/

Joo-Lee's Story

Relax – simple but not easy

To relax sounds so simple; it sounds as though there is nothing to do. And there is nothing to do! We can be so busy doing things, taking action and pushing on to the next part of the journey when in fact it's not so much the doing that we need to do; it's the relaxing.

Why is it not so easy? I think it's because relaxing can make me feel that I am not in control of the events I want to control. The fact of the matter is... we can't control events or the results.

Last weekend, I was rehearsing my dancers and I asked them what they wanted to get out of the performance. One person said, 'I want it to go perfectly.' We have no control over the outcome. We can show up, practice, engage with what we're doing, then relax and let it flow; let it happen.

I use the same relax principle with my dance students, with my music students and with myself! I know that if we don't relax, we can become tense and rigid when dancing or when playing an instrument. I teach the flute and can see what happens when a student tries too hard to play well. Their lips and throat can tense up as a substitute for breathing and letting the breath do the work. If they release tension and allow their lips to form the necessary embouchure the most beautiful sounds will happen. When the desired result doesn't happen immediately it's so tempting to push and force the outcome. Doing this will slow our progress down.

The same goes for the partner dancing that I teach. I use techniques that encourage my students to relax and release whilst keeping the motion and momentum going. It's in relaxing our limbs and releasing our partners that movement is achieved between partners when we improvise to music and respond to each other's' movements.

Yes, to relax sounds almost too simple; but if dancers are focused on learning more moves and execute one fancy move after another, we are not really communicating or connecting with our partner. Instead, I encourage my dancers to practice relaxing and releasing.

Otherwise, we end up having tensed limbs, making everything harder and busier when the experience of social dancing with a partner is so much more rewarding when can let go.

Joo-Lee Stock
www.thedancedoctor.co.uk

Lie Down

Some people don't find success with meditation. If this is your experience, try lying down. I use this method every day as well as meditation. It's my favourite relaxing method!

I personally use the lying-down method when my mind feels overloaded or I'm overwhelmed. If this is what you are feeling, something is out of balance. This is a sign that you need to stop. The first step is to return to balance, as you stop and reset your mind and emotions.

Corpse Pose

Lie on your back on the floor, a yoga mat or a bed. Lay your arms down on your side with your legs straight. Put a pillow under your head for comfort and a pillow under your knees if you have lower back pain. Make yourself comfortable. Pull a blanket up over yourself if you feel cold. Lie quietly and breathe. Observe the process as you inhale and exhale. Your mind will wander, but it will eventually slow. When you catch yourself thinking, invite your focus back into your body, back to your breath. Lie still until you feel your mind slow.

Steps to relaxing lying down:

1) Lie on your back, pillow under your head, pillow under your knees, blanket on top.
2) Breathe—give your mind time and space to process everything going on. It may take time for the mind to settle.
3) Be aware of your thoughts; when you notice your mind thinking about something, bring it back to the moment, and then come back to your breath.

4) Lie still for a minimum of 10 minutes—ideally 20 minutes—until you feel your mind slow down and reset. You may want to set an alarm in case you drift off.

Lying down usually means sleep for your body and mind so just be mindful that there may be a tendency to doze off or even fall asleep in this position. If you need to be somewhere, do set an alarm so you can relax without concern about stopping at that time.

Your body and mind know how to bring you back into balance. Your body knows how to heal itself. Give your mind and body time and space to find that natural harmony again. Your body needs this to rebalance itself each and every day. Taking time to relax is the first step to getting back into your natural abundant flow.

Resistance to Relaxing

These ideas might come up to stop you from making step one a priority:

- Thinking you are too busy.
- Not making time.
- Forgetting.

- Thinking you will do it later.
- Putting all of your tasks before YOU time.
- Putting the needs of others before yours.
- Feeling frazzled and overwhelmed.

What's really going on with your avoidance? Why might you be avoiding relaxing, stopping and being present with yourself? Well, there are many possibilities… for example:

Deeper, unconscious emotions that you don't want to acknowledge

These feelings can be so buried that you don't even know they exist and yet they can be the strong unconscious pull taking you away from the moment, in order to avoid the pain or distress they may bring.

When you stop and simply be, you feel everything

When you still your mind and body, you will be more aware of how you actually feel. We all have coping strategies to avoid feeling. When you stop the activity, there is no hiding. The emotions that you have been unconsciously avoiding may come to the surface.

Feeling uncomfortable

It can feel intense when you relax. It's normal and understandable that there might be a strong drive to get away from that feeling. Avoidance is a protection mechanism. All of your avoidance strategies have been there to keep you safe. So we want to thank that protection and move forward. Your avoidance strategies are getting in the way of changing your life for the better.

Busy patterns are designed to keep you disconnected and not feeling

If you find yourself busy, busy, busy, have an honest conversation with yourself about this. These patterns are tricky because they feel so real and so important. Any anxiety, sense of being overwhelmed or stress you are feeling is a creation of the mind. From this place, everything seems to take top priority! But often when you slow down, you gain greater perspective on what really is important and what you can let go.

Societal patterns of being shut down, being shut off and disconnected

Most people are walking around shut down, shut off and

disconnected. Most people are sleepwalking through their lives. Young children are naturally open, present and in the moment. From a very young age, when everyone else is shut down, you get the message that it's not acceptable to be super conscious and aware. If no one else is being present then you learn to do the same. You learn to shut down too. You have learned this pattern from the society that you live in and from your family. So again, it's not surprising that you might find it challenging to sit with what's really going on if you have never done this before.

We have not been taught the value of being

Have you ever been told that it's valuable to sit and do nothing? We're taught the value of *doing* in our society, not *being*. When you are busy and productive you are considered a contributing member of society. We have not been taught that there's value in sitting and being present with yourself.

Not feeling good enough or worthy

This pattern is acknowledged by every single person with whom I speak. If this pattern is troubling you, consciously or unconsciously, it can also stop you from being present with yourself. If you don't feel good enough or worthy, you may not value making time and space for you. You might keep putting everybody else ahead of you. For example, 'Step 1: Relax' is about loving yourself and valuing yourself enough to create this time and space for you. You are worth it.

These are some of the patterns to watch for because they can be the motivations that stop you from taking time and space for you. It's normal to resist positive change. It's your ego's protection mechanism jumping in and trying to save you from making any detours away from what's safe. As you begin to incorporate these new practices, identify these tendencies, recognise these patterns and don't let them take over.

In challenging moments, it is also important to strengthen your money WHY. Let your WHY be the thing that's going to motivate you to make that time and space for yourself each day.

It is normal to resist 'Step 1: Relax' in the 'Abundance Activation' process. You avoid relaxing because you are ultimately avoiding yourself. There may be emotions, thoughts, beliefs or suppressed pain that you face when you begin this process. When you stop and go within, there is no hiding anymore.

This buried pain that you have been hiding from is

exactly what you need to clear in order to achieve greater financial abundance. I am going to invite you to be courageous, to commit to creating time for you and to trust that this journey is leading you towards your dreams.

The added bonus of relaxing is that it helps you to feel more relaxed! Ultimately, it reduces stress, anxiety, chaos and confusion. It's a form of preventative medicine. There are many health benefits to being more relaxed.

Relaxing is the practice of giving your mind, thoughts and emotions room to re-balance. When you are in balance, your connection with the natural flow of life, your Abundance, is strengthened.

End of Chapter Actions

Register for book bonuses:
http://larawaldman.com/money-manifestation-mastery-book-bonuses/

- Schedule time to relax in your diary every day.
- Commit to a minimum of 20 minutes for 'Step 1: Relax' every day.
- Allow 5 to 10 minutes at night to journal what came up for you in the day around money.

Chapter 3

Step 2: Release

'If you correct your mind, the rest of life will fall into place.'

– Lao Tzu

Releasing is the practice of letting go of all that is blocking your financial abundance: emotionally, mentally, spiritually and energetically. These abundance blocks are made up of the all the negative thoughts, feelings, emotions and beliefs that you absorbed and accepted throughout your life around money.

Your relationship with money is formed by the thoughts, beliefs and emotions that you learned from your family, your ancestors, your friends, your culture, and society, as well as the societal programming from the city that you have been raised in, the country that you were raised in, and also where you live now. Collective consciousness has a strong and often unconscious impact on how you feel, think and behave. Your relationship with money is also made up of any decisions, conclusions and judgments that you have made based on your experience of money as it has appeared in your life.

In order to connect to your natural flow of abundance,

you will need to release all of the points of views, opinions and judgements that are holding you back from creating a positive relationship with money. Here you are going to be exposing these patterns around money and bringing them to the surface in order to let them go. You are going to be releasing everything that stops you from receiving money and all of the good things in life.

Most of your money blocks are running on an unconscious level. Your money blocks are like an iceberg. You are only aware of what is going on, on the top of the money iceberg, but most of what is defining your relationship with money is beneath the surface of the water, which is where most of the iceberg lies.

Your money blocks make it much harder for financial reward to come into your life. Your money blocks put up walls to wealth. You can compare these blocks to hiding underground and wondering why you can't see the sun. You need to remove the walls, the ceiling, the money prison that you have put yourself in in order to experience money manifestation magic.

The great news is that you do not need to carry any of this unconscious junk any longer. Even better news is that it is possible to rid yourself of these negative barriers, once and for all. It is vital for your health, energy and purpose upon this earth that you do.

Releasing your money blocks requires a regular practice of letting go of your negative money mindset if you wish to have a wonderful relationship with abundance and thrive in your life.

You can use this practice of releasing if you feel that you don't have enough in your life and you can use this 'Abundance Activation' practice if you are doing well financially, but you know that more is possible for you and your business. You may want to take your finances to the next level from the energy of ease and joy rather than making money from a place of stress and hard work. There will always be ways that you are holding yourself back. The trick is to see it, release it and open up to achieve an even greater level of abundance.

Money is one of the ways in which you can receive the most beautiful aspects of life. Money is the energy of creation; it is an expression of source energy. Money is a vehicle to experiencing an extraordinary life. Money is a means to experiencing life to the fullest. Money is simply energy from the higher levels of consciousness wanting to express itself in the world. And yet there are many ways you prevent this Universal love and creative energy from coming into your life.

As you go through this process of 'Abundance Activation', it's going to become clearer how much you are blocking from your life and why it's important to keep releasing the beliefs and thoughts that stop you from experiencing a life of greater ease, joy and abundance.

The practices you are learning are powerful but also simple. Releasing money blocks does not need to be difficult. It does not need to be painful. You simply want to keep letting go of anything that is stopping you from receiving the good things in life, money included.

Money Mindset

Your money mindset is the core of your relationship with money and how money is showing up in your life. A negative money mindset prevents money from flowing into your life with ease. Any success you have with your relationship with finances originates from a positive money mindset. Most of the *work* to change your relationship with money for the better lies in shifting your negative money mindset and lifting the lid on where you limit your success and abundance.

You may not be able to see where you are successful with money, as most often we don't notice what is working in our lives. Humans tend to default to focusing on the negative. As we will mainly be working with your negative money mindset in this step, it's worth taking time to think about what is working in your life when it comes to finances.

Take a moment to journal on, *'What is working in my life right now?'*

Your natural state is abundance, your true nature is abundance, so what blocks this? You do! Blocking your natural flow of abundance mostly happens on an unconscious level. The practices I am sharing with you are designed to help you identify and dislodge your money blocks so you can live your intended flow of financial abundance.

What are some of the 'Money Mindset' pitfalls that you may be prone to? There are various combinations of beliefs around money all mixed up together which you may be basing your decisions on, knowingly or unknowingly, but here are some of the money blocks pulled apart so we can examine them separately. You will have your own unique blend of these, which you will uncover over time in this 'Abundance Activation' process. You may be very aware of some of your money blocks and some of them may take you by surprise. It is always fascinating uncovering what is going on for you unconsciously when it comes to your relationship with money and abundance.

Why is it Important to Release?

These money blocks—your limiting thoughts, beliefs, emotions and programming around money—are hiding your truth. They are covering up your light. They put up a shade to who you are and block out the brightness of your soul. Your money blocks are hiding the truth of your being, your true essence, your higher self, your soul.

When I refer to soul, higher self, infinite being, true self, true essence, I am referring to the same thing—the truth of you.

Negativity and heaviness are not the truth of who you are. They are very much a part of our human experience, but not on the level of your higher self. These money blocks are like energetic weights limiting what is possible for your life.

'Abundance Activation' is about connecting you to the real impact that I believe you were born to make and why you chose to be here on this planet at this time. These money blocks hide the truth of who you are, limit your full potential and limit your impact in the world.

Life has so much more to offer you. It has so much more to offer all of us. It is possible to enjoy life and for life to be a joyful experience. I believe we are here to experience life to the fullest, the expression of being in a body and living on this planet. Having this physical experience is extraordinary. These hindrances limit how much you can experience this joy.

Imagine you are on an airplane. You are in this amazing vehicle that is transporting you to a new land, a new way of being. On this journey, you are going to be invited to release and let go of all the old fears, the old paradigm, to allow yourself to arrive in this new, wonderful place. With this 'Abundance Activation' process, you are creating a new paradigm of experiencing life on this planet.

The old paradigm of living, what you thought life was, is not serving you anymore. It's been holding you back for too long now.

Signs that you Need to Release

How do you recognise your money blocks? What are the signs that you have money barriers you need to release? What can you look for?

Very simply, any kind of negativity is a sign that something within is preventing your ability to believe there is more. This could appear in negative thoughts, negative words, negative feelings. Any thoughts, words, or feelings that simply don't feel good need to be released.

Having low energy, feeling heavy, depressed, anxious, overwhelmed, frustrated, angry, in lack, essentially anything that doesn't feel good indicates that you have blocks. These negative feelings won't be about money alone, but they will impact your relationship with money and abundance.

Releasing is not about perfection. This isn't about never having *bad* feelings ever again. Not at all. Having emotions, of all kinds, is part of being human. You will have unhappiness, you will have challenging times, this is all normal. But when you find yourself in a negative, heavy state of being, you can make the choice to move back into feeling good again, to step into a higher vibration, to connect back to your truth. Negative energy is a sign that something within yourself needs your attention. It's simply a way for your mind, emotions and body to communicate with you.

Your truth is aligned with feeling good, balanced, peaceful, clear, positive, powerful, alive and in flow. When you are in a negative state of being, it simply means that there is something within yourself that needs redirection.

Releasing is a process. This is a practice. If you are blocked, heavy or down it does not mean that you have failed.

Imagine you are driving along and one of the lights starts flashing in your car indicating that you are getting low on fuel or that the battery strength is low. This is simply a sign saying that something in the car needs your attention so that this vehicle can function optimally. It does not mean that the car is useless or has failed. It just alerts you to take some action. Your negative emotions, your heavy energy are signals from yourself that something within yourself needs your attention.

From my personal and professional experience, releasing is a daily practice. Feeling good and aligned to your higher self, staying in the flow of abundance, is a choice you make on a daily and often moment-to-moment basis.

What is Blocking you from Receiving Money?

I'd like you to think about your WOW goal. What is that WOW goal? This is an amount of money that makes you feel financially free, relaxed and at ease. It can be a sum you bring in monthly or annually, and it can also be a sum that is sitting in your wealth pot. What are you asking for?

You are now going to ask your intuition to show you what is stopping you from welcoming in your WOW goal now. Take a deep breath, close your eyes, think of your

WOW goal and then ask:

'What is preventing me from welcoming this money into my life now?'

What comes up for you? It may be a feeling, a thought, a memory, a visual image. What's the first thing that appears to you? Write the answer down in your money journal.

What can Appear when Releasing?

When you start digging into your money blocks and take a closer look at what it is that's holding you back from accepting money into your life, what shows up are deep patterns that you may not even be aware of running inside of you. I definitely wasn't aware of a lot of these patterns when I first started on my money manifestation journey.

Here is a list of the most common money blocks that I have come across when working with clients:

- Low self-worth.
- Not feeling good enough.
- Feeling undeserving.
- Fear of rejection.
- Fear of being judged.
- Feeling alone.

- Feeling un-loveable.
- Feeling something is wrong with you.
- Afraid to be seen.
- Money = responsibility.
- Fear of responsibility.
- Not trusting yourself.
- Not feeling safe.
- Believing you have to work hard for money.
- In order to make more money, you have to work harder.
- Feeling guilty if you have money or good things in life.
- Feeling greedy if you have money.
- Feeling undeserving of money or good things in life.
- A belief that if you have money others will go without—if you gain, others lose.
- Believing you are not a good person.
- You will lose your friends and family if you have money.
- Money = no love or attention.
- Fear of success.
- Fear of being too much.
- Neglecting money.
- Vow of poverty.
- Worrying about money.

- You will be hurt if you have money.
- You will be rejected.
- You will abandon others if you have money.

These are the common themes coming up again and again for people, especially the women with whom I speak. Which of these resonate with you? When you dig beneath the surface of what you believe, you will discover at least a couple of the above patterns dictating your reasoning and belief system.

All of these feelings and beliefs you have about money feel real. This is the truth, right? Wrong! These are simply your *thoughts and beliefs* about money, your *thoughts and beliefs* about yourself, not the truth.

Your *thoughts and beliefs* create your reality. So yes, they are real as long as you buy into them. Your *thoughts and beliefs* about wealth create your financial reality. So if you want to change that, you need to change your money mindset. It really is as simple as that.

It's time to shift this now; it's time to release the feeling that you are not allowed to have a great life, in all areas, with ease and joy. Life doesn't have to be as hard and painful as you are making it.

With 'Step 2: Release', you will be shining a loving spotlight on these aspects of yourself, these shadow beliefs, the parts of you that are hidden, so you can release them and set them free.

When you set these money blocks free you will uncover the gold waiting for you. There is always gold to be found in your greatest challenges. That's why this work is so rewarding. There are great gifts that will come in your greatest struggles and pain.

The gift that you are uncovering is who you truly are and what you have come here on this planet to be, share and experience. You are exploring the cave that is you. You are shining a light in the dark places within, unlocking and exposing all that's preventing your magnificence, your greatness, your power, preventing you from standing strong in who you are and sharing all that you have come to give.

Uncovering the truth of you is the true purpose of this 'Abundance Activation' work. Put simply, being in the flow of abundance makes living on this planet so much more enjoyable.

The practice of changing your money mindset is simple, and the tools that I am teaching you here are very simple. The challenge is in remembering to release your money blocks and to stop buying into your negative money mindset as reality.

The tools in this book work if you use them. All that is

required of you is the commitment to your dreams and taking action to make your dreams materialise. Commit to a different choice around money and then act on it.

If you are struggling to believe that these tools work, why don't you approach this as a great experiment? Put these abundance activation tools to the test. Does this work? Let's see how shifting your money mindset impacts how much money you receive into your life. Let's play!

Niamh's Story

Self-Worth and Value

Lara's work with 'Abundance Activation' is truly life changing. The work around money manifestation is vast and multifaceted in a way I would never have imagined. If I am honest, I am shocked at the scope and depth of this body of work. For me working on my relationship with money was like holding a mirror up to all aspects of my life. This of course is challenging but ultimately profoundly freeing.

In my case going on this journey with Lara, was about learning to deeply value my work and myself on a new level. Her work has allowed me to begin to let my true colours shine through and that is a big difference to how I thought about value and valuing myself before.

In the past, I would value myself for my achievements, or for the worth I am creating or for going jogging, or, for how nice I was as a friend. Now I am learning to value myself for who I truly am and for what I truly desire. This has magical effects. As I allow my work to flow from that place, so many questions and anxieties around what I am doing or how I am doing it have fallen away. Because I feel so much more in alignment with my work, it has become far easier to steer my business in the right direction. I am allowing my business to unfold as it wants to and I can just go along for the ride. In the past month, I have tripled my number of private clients effortlessly. They just come knocking! This way of working and the kind of work I am doing now, is so easy and enjoyable for me that I feel a bit like I am being paid to be myself.

Niamh Mckernan
Movement Teacher, Director, Coach and Bodyworker
www.niamhmckernan.com

Money Mindset Mop Out

How do you change these negative thoughts and beliefs? How do you create a different reality around money?

In order to change your money mindset, you need to make time on a regular basis to clear out and let go of all the emotions, past pain, judgements, thoughts and belief systems centered on finances that are holding you back.

I recommend spending a couple of minutes each day at the end of your meditation session for this 'Money Mindset Mop Out'. You do not need to know exactly what your money blocks are to let them go. You simply need to be *willing* to let them go.

As you do this simple practice, you will become more aware and conscious of the belief systems and emotions that are holding you back around accepting abundance.

How to Release

The first step in releasing your money blocks is to identify your limiting thoughts and beliefs, those you are conscious of, at least. You are not going to be aware of all of them at first. Your money blocks will reveal themselves to you as you continue through this process on your abundance activation journey.

There is a lot going on within your unconscious. Remember the iceberg I mentioned before. You are aware of the tip of the iceberg but there is so much more going on in the unconscious, underneath the surface of the water.

For now, you can identify the limiting thoughts and beliefs you are aware of, knowing that as you progress on this journey, more and more will come to you as you follow the abundance activation steps.

Anytime you go up a level in your life, in your business, anytime that you ask for more money, anytime you are stretching beyond your comfort zone, your money blocks are going to show up. This can be very uncomfortable. My hope for you is that eventually you will learn to trust in this process through dedicated practice and experience.

Identify your controlling thoughts and beliefs, those you are conscious of having. Then you want to be mindful of how these limiting thoughts, beliefs and emotions appear throughout the day.

Your money mindset will reveal itself to you many times throughout the day. Bring your awareness and your attention to this process.

Your attention is powerful. Your attention brings a spotlight of awareness to you and your money blocks, which will create space for you to let go of these blocks.

Be mindful about what you say out loud to others and what you say to yourself. Start watching your thoughts and your words. If your thoughts and your words are not in alignment with abundance and manifesting greater wealth into your life, don't say them.

For example, from now on, never say, *'I can't afford it'* again. Make this pact with yourself. Reframe, *'I can't afford it'* to, *'All the money that I need is coming to me now'*, or, *'I choose not to invest in that right now'*.

Staying Out of the Story

Whatever thought or memory comes that is restrictive, no matter how difficult or painful it is, stay out of the story. Try not to go into the story of your past pain or past hurt. Don't go into the financial story of your past or what is showing up for you now in your present financial reality.

What happened to you in your past and what is showing up for you in your present is real, but you want to move beyond your story, you want to move beyond your past reality as you have experienced it up until now, and shift into a more empowered state of being.

Your mind will want to hold onto the story and fixate on the pain, recount details from the past. The ego mind wants to make sense of your feelings so it will grab onto any evidence presenting itself. This can result in what I call 'looping' where you mind goes around and around the same details over and over again. This keeps you a slave to your past.

You have the power to change your past, you have the power to change the story of what your life has been so far, you have the power to change your present and create the future that you truly desire. You have the power to create a new future reality starting now. Don't take your past pain into your future or you will create a future based on your past.

It is not always easy to stay out of the story of your past or present. We are storytellers and humans are drawn to drama. Staying out of the story is a discipline. You will go into your past or present and buy into it as real, but when you find yourself starting to do that, catch yourself and focus on what you actually want to create for your future.

For example, you may have had a very difficult past when it comes to money, or you may be struggling now with money. In order to change your financial reality in the future, you want to focus on what you want moving forward, not on the struggle of your past or present. Acknowledge it, honour it, and then redirect your mind to envision what you want.

Observe your money blocks. You want to watch them, notice them without any judgement. Judging your money blocks only keeps them firmly in place. Ideally you want to love and accept these parts of you, see them for what they are, then from the energy of acceptance, make the decision to let them go.

Letting go of your barriers to wealth is about letting go of your old story, letting go of the past, letting go of your attachments to pain, to suffering, to lack and limitation. Most people are addicted to those limiting states of being. It's time to let go of the addiction to pain and suffering.

If you have experienced these feelings in your life, they can become your comfort zone. I don't mean that pain and suffering is comfortable, but it's what you know as reality. Therefore, transforming your life into what you truly want is about releasing anything negative you are unconsciously creating or being drawn to in your life.

Staying in pain and suffering can become a *bad* habit. It's time to reprogramme this old way of being into what you truly desire. As strange as this may sound, if you have known such despair in your life, peace, joy, freedom and happiness can be uncomfortable.

Releasing your money blocks is a journey, it is a daily practice. You are practicing being mindful. With 'Step 2: Release', you are practicing watching your thoughts and your words. You are inviting yourself to stay out of your story. You are inviting yourself to observe your money blocks, to accept these parts of you, to love these parts of you, then make the choice to no longer hold onto them. It's time to set your money blocks free.

Are you ready for a very simple way of clearing your limiting money mindset? It's almost too easy. So easy you may even dismiss it as ineffective. I promise you this works, even if you don't *feel* it working. You need to be willing to change your mind, your mindset.

Are you ready? Are you ready for releasing money blocks to be easy?

Money Mindset Mop Out

After 'Step 1: Relax', at the end of the 20 minutes of breathing and being present with yourself, simply say:

'*I give myself permission to let go of everything and anything that is blocking me from experiencing financial abundance. I release anything and everything that is blocking money from flowing into my life now. I set it free now.*'

When you say this, imagine all of the barriers to financial freedom melting out of your mind and body into the earth beneath you and out into the universe. Know that these hindrances to having money will all be transformed as you release them.

The most important thing here is not the words you say, but the intention behind the words. You need to mean what you say! You need to fully embody what you are saying.

You need to be willing to let go of everything that holds you back from experiencing financial abundance.

Letting go is a process and doesn't all happen instantly, but the more you practice, the more aligned to abundance you will be.

Give yourself permission to step into a new financial reality. This will take you to an experience with money beyond your family, beyond the experience of your ancestors and beyond the society you live in. Be prepared, open and willing to begin a whole new relationship with money, one you've never known before.

If you can't feel anything releasing, ask yourself:

'What is the value of holding on to all of this? Would I be willing to let that go now?'

If you make space daily for this 'Money Mindset Mop Out', you will make space for more and more financial abundance to come into your life over time. This is a daily practice, not a quick fix. These old money blocks can take time to shift once and for all. You may let go in the moment but old habitual ways of being, thinking and feeling can creep back in. This is why it's important to keep practicing these steps every day.

I see releasing as similar to cleaning. You may clean your house from top to bottom. Your house, just after it's been cleaned, looks and feels amazing, but after a few days, dirt will start to accumulate. Just because you vacuum or mop the floor once doesn't mean that you won't have to do it again fairly soon. You need to clean and tidy your house regularly to keep it clean and tidy. The same goes for your mindset, emotions, thoughts and beliefs. The negative mindset patterns need to be cleared on a regular basis.

Releasing Techniques

The most vital part of releasing your money blocks is your intention. In a way, it doesn't matter how you do it, whether you like talking to angels, burning sage or dancing in your living room. Whatever it is, it's not so much the vehicle of releasing that is important but your decision to free your mind of whatever stops you from achieving financial gain.

I'm all about making things as simple as possible. I want to give you tools you can use in any moment of any day because you can't always wave your sage stick around, or it may not always be possible to dance around, do your screaming or whatever your releasing techniques may be.

My releasing technique is simple and it works well. The power comes in believing what you are saying. You need to fully commit to what you are saying and what you intend to let go.

You can also say this:

'All of the limiting energies, thoughts, beliefs, emotions and programming that stop me or block me from receiving this money into my life with ease and joy, I let them go now.' Make sure you mean what you say: *'I release them. I'm willing to set them free now.'*

Say this statement every day. The words are not the most important part; rather, it's your intention behind the words. The power is in your willingness to release anything and everything that's preventing you from welcoming in all of the beautiful energies of the Universe, this money, that's waiting for you. The power is in your choice to change.

Every time you speak this releasing intention, every time you intend to let go, you are chipping away at your money blocks. Sometimes you can blast them all at once, but there may be areas of thought that are more firmly embedded, areas where your ego is clinging a little tighter. But, as you hold fast to your decision to release your money blocks, you will allow yourself to manifest more money into your life.

It's similar to forging a new path in an overgrown forest. In the process of blazing this new path, you may my reactive feelings shift and balance again.

Sometimes your negative beliefs will shift within a few minutes but sometimes it takes longer. Eventually, if you remain silent, breathing for long enough, they will pass.

Releasing is about letting go of what no longer serves you. This is an ongoing process. As much as possible, celebrate the journey. As much as you can, make the most of the process. This is not about reaching a final destination.

The truth is, there is no finish line. So, enjoy the view as you go along on your money manifestation journey.

What Stops You from Releasing

What stops you from releasing? All of these concepts and practices are super simple, but there can be deeper matters that come up again and again that stop you in your tracks. This is where our lovely friend, the ego, often makes an appearance. I also refer to your ego as your small self or your limiting self.

I have spent a lot of time working with egos during my years as a Healer. Over the years, I have created a loving relationship with 'the ego' that I would like to share with you here.

Your ego is designed to keep you safe, that's its job.

Your ego wants to keep you where you are now because where you are is what you know. The ego says, 'This is what we know. This is okay. It might not be great but at least we are familiar with what this is. We are safer here.'

When you start stepping beyond what you know, the ego has a strong reaction and will respond by shouting, 'Danger! Danger! Alert! Alert! Do not continue! Do not step forward.' The ego's job is to keep you protected. It's like an overprotective parent that won't let you explore the world. There has been a place for your ego, you have needed it until now. But your ego is getting in the way and limiting you in creating positive change.

How to work with your Ego

Do you remember those old cartoons with an angel sitting on one side of a character's shoulders, and a devil on the other? The angel is whispering to be good and kind, while the devil is saying to be naughty and bad. I liken the ego to the devil, and your higher self, or your soul, to the angel. Your higher self embodies freedom and infinite possibilities, abundance, joy and love.

When you are about to do something that is going to change your life, like welcoming in more money, for example, your little ego devil starts conjuring up all sorts of suggestions to stop you from moving out of the world that you know. It may sound something like this: *'Do not continue, this is dangerous. Are you mad? Are you crazy? You're going to fail. Don't do this, you're delusional. You are not good enough, you are not qualified!'*

When this happens, you can strengthen the voice of your angel or your higher self and soften the grip of your ego. Now, I'm not sure if it's possible to eliminate the ego altogether. But all that is needed now is to strengthen your connection to source, to your higher self, so that this becomes the determining force within you. You can then recognise when the ego voice is trying to take over and stop it.

How Does the Ego Speak to You?

You are very, very familiar with how your ego speaks to you. You have heard it many times. Your ego voice is the negative, fear-based, limiting voice in your head that feels so real and true. They are all the unhappy things you say to yourself constantly but you may be unconscious of these thoughts or buying into them as real and true. These voices feel like the truth, which is what makes them so sly and difficult to identify at times. They will sound something like, *'I'm not good enough. I'm not worthy. I can't do it. I don't know how. I'm not ready. I'm going to fail. I'm going to be rejected.'*

Your ego creates separation and competition with others. Your ego can leave you feeling alone and cut off from others. Your ego instills inferiority complexes or superiority complexes. It can leave you feeling less than others or better than others. Beware of that ego wreaking havoc in your thoughts and in your interactions with others.

Any negative or limiting voice is the voice of your ego self. That's how you can identify it. Your higher self, your soul, never speaks to you in dark or fearful voices.

Hello Ego

The first step in stripping the ego of its power over you is to stop buying into what you are hearing as the truth, see it for what it is. Recognise that it's your ego voice speaking, and you're not bound by it. You then want to release it.

I would like to share with you a technique to lower the sound of your ego voice. When I'm working with clients, I see and feel when their ego self pops up. The ego comes up to fight or resist the releasing process. The ego appears when change is on the horizon and creates resistance. This is the resistance to letting go into the unknown, to taking positive action. When you are inviting yourself to expand into a new way of being, your friend the ego will show up to stop the process.

When this happens, I talk to the ego. I would like to teach you how you can talk to your ego. I see the ego like a bodyguard. You can imagine your ego as if its purpose is to keep you safe and protected. When you are doing this process for yourself it may help to write the answers that come up for you in your journal.

'Hello, ego. I can feel you are really concerned here. Tell me more about it. What's going on? What are you worried about?'

Then listen to what your Ego has to say.

Writing the answers in your journal will help focus your attention. After your ego has expressed all of its worries and concerns, then you say:

'Yes, I get that, I can feel that. I understand your point.'

I listen to the Ego, I hear it, I acknowledge it. I will say something along the lines of:

'Yes, that is perfectly understandable, that makes sense. Tell me more.'

I talk to the ego about its fears, doubts, anger or concerns until it runs out of things to say. Then when the ego part of you feels heard, it will start to relax. Your ego will begin to drop its guard because this part of you has been acknowledged and heard.

Keep an open dialogue going. You can continue by saying:

'Yes, I hear you. I can really see that logic.'

And then I'll say something along the lines of:

'I appreciate you're trying to keep me safe. I'm so thankful to you. You have done such a good job of keeping me from harm. Thank you! I really needed you up until now.'

You have depended on this part of you; this part of you has been here for a reason. Your ego has been there to protect you.

You can then go on to say:

'But the trouble is, ego, I now want to experience financial freedom, I want to welcome more money into my life with ease and joy. I wonder what my life would look like, be like, feel like with all this money coming into my life? The problem is that you are blocking this from happening. You are getting in the way of this experience. So, I'm wondering if you wouldn't mind stepping aside for a while. Take a holiday, have a rest. You have been working so hard. You can relax a little, take a back seat and I will call you if I need you.'

When I'm working with a client's ego, it will start saying something along the lines of:

'This is my job. You're trying to stop me from performing my duties here.'

And so I'll talk to the ego and say:

'Look, you deserve a rest. You have been working way too hard for way too long now. Just take a seat over on the side here. You don't have to go anywhere. You can jump in the second I need you.'

The ego is like an overprotective bodyguard who takes his job way too seriously. You simply want to soothe your ego, calm the fear. I find that talking to the ego is one way to reassure it.

You can journal with your ego or sit and meditate with it. Whatever works best for you. You might be surprised by what comes up.

My practice is to love the ego, to acknowledge it and be thankful for it, because it has a purpose, it has a job. Your ego just goes overboard at times, especially when you are moving out of what is familiar, into the unfamiliar.

Letting Go of Control

Letting go is about going into the unknown. The unknown can be scary! You need to be willing to give up control, to step into unchartered territory on this journey to financial freedom. This can be frightening.

Releasing your negative money mindset is all about letting go of everything that no longer serves you. Sometimes this is hard for your mind to accept, so be patient.

Make a note of the limiting thoughts and beliefs you have around finances and where they came from. Observe your relationship with money and keep clearing those patterns that no longer serve you. If your current mindset doesn't lead to financial freedom, then it's time to set it free.

As you change your money mindset, you will change. We often mistakenly identify with who we are based on how we think and feel. What if how you think and feel is not the full picture of who you truly are?

Stepping away from the old can be scary and uncomfortable because you are stepping away from who you thought you were, what you thought life was. To your poor ego this can feel like a death.

Moving into a new reality, a new way of being, takes courage and faith. You need to be willing to surrender what is no longer working for you and accept this new reality.

Please remember that the Universe has your back. The Universe loves you unconditionally and wants the very best for you and your life. You are supported in this process. The next step is to open up to receive!

Your Invisible Helpers

You have support in this 'Abundance Activation' process on the other levels of consciousness. I experience these energetic helpers as spirit guides, angels, ancestors, energies from the Earth and other beautiful beings and energies that we can't see with our physical eyes (unless you are clairvoyant!). The Universe wants to help you create your life for the better. Call on these invisible helpers to help as you let go of everything that no longer serves you. You can ask:

'Please help me release everything and anything that is no longer beneficial to me. Help me to clear out everything that is blocking me from experiencing financial abundance. Help me to step into my true financially abundant nature.'

This energetic help comes the moment you ask for it. Ask and you shall receive! All you need is there instantly on an energetic level, but it can take time to show up in the physical. Keep asking and be patient. Everything that you request is coming to you now.

Judgements

How many judgements do you have running your life? I will tell you right now that you have many. Judgements can be both positive and negative. You can judge someone to be bad and unkind or you can judge someone to be good and kind. In both cases judgements block out the full picture, the full truth. When you judge someone to be bad and unkind, you block yourself from seeing any other possibility. You demonise them. This makes it difficult to see any *good* in them. Even kind action will go unnoticed. If you judge someone to be kind and good, equally this may block you from seeing the full picture of what is going on. Maybe there are aspects of this person that aren't always so kind. You want to have a full awareness of what is and keep your eyes wide open. Your judgements cloud your perception of what is possible for you and your life.

Our society is riddled with judgements. Judgements create separation, loneliness, disappointment, fights and even war. So much of the destruction on our planet comes from judgements.

You can't get away from judgements in the world but you can bring your awareness to your own judgements and make a choice to release them. What do these beliefs create for your reality? Watch and observe. You will realise just how much pain judgements create in our world.

Releasing your judgements will not only make your life more enjoyable and allow greater ease in your everyday interactions, it will also open up many doors for you. Your judgements block out the infinite possibilities for good that are available to you. Make the choice to keep releasing them.

'I release all the judgements I am carrying now. I let them all go.'

End of Chapter Actions

- Register for the book bonus material here: http://larawaldman.com/money-manifestation-mastery-book-bonuses/
- Run 'Step 1: Relax' and 'Step 2: Release' every day.
- Watch your thoughts, watch your words.
- Release all limiting thoughts and beliefs throughout the day when you catch them, then come back to your WOW GOAL and your money FUEL.
- Talk to your ego.
- Journal on:
  - *What is money to you?*
  - *How do you feel about money?*
  - *What does money mean to you?*

- *How do your parents feel about money? Family? Friends?*
- *What does it mean to be wealthy?*
- *When you become financially free, what will this mean for your life?*
- *What is working for you in your relationship with money? What's going well when it comes to money?*

These questions will help to reveal some of your beliefs around money and the money mindset that may be holding you back.

Chapter 4

Step 3: Receive

'Abundance is not something we acquire, it's something we tune into.'

– Wayne Dyer

Receiving is your willingness to allow support, love, help, abundance, happiness, joy, health and wealth. It's your ability to receive all of what life has to offer, including the great things in life. Receiving is your willingness to accept from the Universe and everything that life wants to give you. In this book, we are focusing specifically on financial abundance and money but these principles apply to all that you want in every area of your life.

This next step is about receiving money into your life in alignment with your higher self or soul. These 'Abundance Activation' steps are teaching you about money manifestation with ease.

Most people actively and unconsciously block themselves from receiving. This happens for all sorts of reasons, such as low self-worth, not feeling good enough, fear and not feeling safe. Blocking yourself from abundance is a way of protecting yourself from the world.

It is essential that you open up to all of the love,

support, energy, abundance, health and money that is waiting for you if you wish to experience a life of greater ability and joy.

The Universe loves you and is gifting you in every second of every day. All you need to do is breathe in this love and let the Universal gifts flow to you. There is an abundant supply of everything that your heart and soul is asking for waiting to come into your life now.

It is your divine nature to be in a state of receiving. You simply need to drop your energetic walls and barriers to abundance and then all that you are asking for will begin to enter into your life.

Receiving is being in divine flow with your higher self and the Universe. It's impossible not to be plugged in to the Universe and to your soul. It's part of who you are. Your connection to source, to the Universe is your life-force connection.

Any lack that is showing up in your life is not in alignment with your true essence. If you are experiencing lack, you are blocking your source connection somehow. You are preventing yourself from receiving somewhere. This is not an opportunity to be hard on yourself. Experiencing blocks, lack or limitation is part of our human experience. Simply use the lack or scarcity in your life as a sign that something needs your attention.

On this planet, we experience duality and separation. The good news is that it's possible to change this experience of duality and separation in your life now. You have the ability to choose something different for yourself and your life. This is the process of reconnecting back to your true essence, to your true connection with source energy. This is the process of creating your life from a conscious, soul-led place.

When receiving, you are welcoming in the good things in life. You are allowing yourself to welcome in money into your life. You have created a variety of energies that stop you from letting life in, which is what 'Step 2: Release' is all about. Receiving is opening up and letting in that flow of Universal love, support and abundance.

What are you receiving? You are opening up to having more of the good in life such as:

- Support
- Help
- Joy
- Pleasure
- Love
- Friendship
- Gifts
- Things that bring you joy

- Time/Space
- Money

Money is the energy of joy, expansion, freedom, play, abundance, fun, sexuality, and power. Money is an energy of creation. You have the ability to create money, to manifest money, to bring more money into your life. You are able to do this. We are now going to awaken your ability to become a 'Money Manifestation Master'.

When receiving, you need to be open to receiving all of life, bringing down your barriers to what life offers and releasing your judgements about life. Without realising it, you have been protecting yourself from life with your energetic barriers and judgements. The trouble is that you are blocking out what you are seeking. This protection needs to come down in order to have what you truly desire.

What may feel like protection to your ego self is not truly benefitting you, as it comes in the form of energetic barriers. In fact, you have put yourself in a type of prison. The walls *protect* you to a degree but they keep you separated from life and what you have come to this planet to experience.

Your true protection comes from your light, from fully showing up and being here in the truth of who you are.

You do not need barricades in the way that the ego feels you do. You are safe. It is okay to be open and let your light shine.

Consciously Creating Your Life

You are powerful beyond measure. You have the power and the ability to create your life. In fact, you do create your life. Whatever is showing up in your life now is your creation. Consciously or unconsciously you have designed your life as it is now, the good, the bad, the wonderful, and the ugly.

The challenge is that most of what you are creating is unconscious. Most of what you have been manifesting is happening on a deeper level of your being that you may not be consciously connected to. You unconsciously form your life from the level of your ego, your pain body, from the experiences of your past, from the experiences of your ancestors, from the society you were raised in and from the society you live in now. This is why we spend so much time releasing these unconscious patterns in 'Step 2: Release'.

You also unconsciously create your life from the level of your soul or higher self. This is a level of creation that becomes harder to speak about as it's so far removed from what our conscious self is aware of, but very simply, your soul is here to have an experience upon this earth. The things that are important to you on a personality level are usually not important to your higher self.

In my work with many souls over the years, I have learned that your higher self wants to realise itself in physical form. It's here to experience all that life has to offer through the vehicle of your body. Your soul is here to have a physical experience. Your soul wants to share and express its essence, its true nature, here upon this earth.

Some believe Earth is like a school. It's a place for the soul to come and experience what it can't experience in other realms of consciousness. On Earth, we have duality, pain and struggle in a way that we don't have beyond this physical dimension. Here on Earth you also can experience the joy of being in a physical body. There are many wonderful, positive experiences to be found in being here on this planet.

Lysa's Story

My journey to allowing myself to receive abundance came as I truly comprehended what was of true value in life.

I received the regular scarcity training that we all

experience to some degree. You can't have the lovely things you want and you're not allowed to go because it costs too much. I saw lack of money as an inhibitor of my freedom and I chose to disregard money in an act of rebellion.

Fast forward 10 years and I had firstly fallen in love with myself, and had now attracted love. My true love had found me and was adoring, devoted and honourable.

We did what we needed to find our way forward, we held little regard for money and used it frivolously or with little joy. Along came our first child and an awareness of all the debt we had accumulated. In our rebellious disregard for money we cut our living expenses and chained ourselves to high repayments.

Those early child-rearing years were hard, yet I took pride in my 'I can do it without you money' self-reliant attitude. But it was a LOT of work! I built a business around service and began learning about making money, so long as I didn't make too much. Three years later and I had mastered my art of giving, my business was full with a steady stream of clients, but my receiving was grossly outmatched. Along came my second child; this time I gave birth to a little girl and all of my money pain came rushing to the surface. My grudge against money suddenly shifted as I realised my position would incriminate my daughter to the life I had created.

I began shifting my relationship with money, learning how to hold it, honour it, appreciate it, talking to it lovingly, entreating it in a way that would reflect my new found devotion and hope for my daughter's future. Love and commitment sure have a way of nourishing all things, and within a year my business had experienced a new all-time level of abundance and high quality service that I was booked out to high paying deeply appreciative clients.

I witnessed how those who invested more in working within, gave more to themselves and the outcomes they wanted to create. I realised that I was still giving more than I was allowing myself to receive and the energetic imbalance took a massive toll. I was tired, I was forever 'working' and began neglecting myself and my family. My husband and I had finally reached a place where our income was over and above our living costs. It was the first time in our 8-year marriage and we sat back and day-dreamed about how we could 'spend' our new found wealth.

That overseas cruise, new tech gadgets, up-grades to our life style all held appeal until we realised that my income was sufficient to allow my husband to decrease his work hours from 40 to 32 hours a week. Yes, that was the most valuable thing our new money could buy, and we re-

arranged my husband's employment to give us more time together. It wasn't long before his 4-day week became a 3-day week and as we lay looking at the clouds feeling the richness of the love that was always ours we knew we needed more. So we set an intention for him to resign in 6 months and re-arrange my business and our lifestyle so that we could invest in being together.

Four weeks later my husband was made redundant, and while we were tempted for 5 minutes to bemoan our new circumstances, instead we cheered and two arms flew into the air as we did a massive high five for our speedy manifesting powers!

Intuitively, we found a new accommodating home, relocated our small family to the country and started living the truly abundant lifestyle and experience of richness we didn't know money could buy. Fast forward 9 months and our family has adjusted and settled into the most connected, expansive and joyful time of our lives. I was prompted to raise my rates again and once again attracted a flurry of willing appreciative clients. I hold money as sacred; it's a means by which I understand the true value of everything in life and by holding it in love and honour I open myself to utilising it to create true joy and freedom.

Lysa Black

Heart Healer

http://www.heartmagic.co.nz

Your Purpose

Humans can get hung up about their purpose and what they are supposed to be doing in their life. Somewhere inside there may be a feeling, an awareness that you are here for a reason, that there is a purpose for your life. From my work on the soul level, I have learned that you don't have a purpose in the way that you think you do, as there isn't one specific job that is the reason for your existence. What I see in my practice is that there may be one vehicle you think is best suited for the expression of your soul, but there are, in fact, many ways to realise your soul's purpose here on this planet.

For example, I called myself a Healer for 13 years. Being a Healer was a great way for me to express my soul's essence. But there could be a number of jobs that similarly worked to that end. I could have also been a singer or a massage therapist, but for 13 years, being a Healer was the best expression for my being. This role has been the best match for my gifts.

My soul has now led me to expand beyond the role of a Healer. I have been led to public speaking, writing books, leading groups and running live events. There are many ways that your soul can express itself, but there may be a few vehicles that will suit you best.

Your soul, your higher self, your true essence, is the all-seeing, all-knowing, infinite part of yourself. This part of who you are is hard for the mind to grasp so it works best by feeling what I am writing about here. As I write, I will ask your higher self to connect to you so that you have a feeling experience of what I am conveying. I am all about feeling your way through life.

Your soul is infinite. There is no beginning or end to your soul. I personally have the great honour of connecting to the soul or higher self of my clients while I work with them. It is the most incredible and humbling experience.

Your soul is perfection. This part of you is tapped into Universal wisdom, Universal knowledge, and has many great gifts. You will already be tapped into some of these parts of you but there is always more to discover!

It is my aim to help you work in harmony with your higher self and your personality self. Your personality self is what you identify with as you. My personality self is Lara and includes my past, my family and my physical life. The soul self is different. It's beyond time and space; it's beyond this physical dimension. Your higher self functions on a completely different level of reality. This part of you is tapped into multi-dimensional realities and is not limited to your physical experience.

In this book, I am guiding you to experience a soul-led life and business. My personal experience, drawn from my own life and from supporting many clients over the years, is that a soul-led life and business results in greater ease, flow and joy. When you work in harmony with your soul, everything in your physical life will also come into harmony.

Your soul has its own reason for being here on this planet. Your soul has come here to have certain experiences through the vehicle of your physical body. Most of the problems in your life arise when you are in resistance to your soul's path. Your ego, or personality self, will have its own agenda. Your ego agenda can take you off on all sorts of unhelpful tangents. If you get too far off course from the experience that your soul wants to have, you will get what I lovingly call 'a bitch slap from the Universe'.

Getting a 'bitch slap from the Universe' is a humorous way of explaining a Universal wake-up call, but sometimes that's what it can feel like! It can feel painful and challenging when you get the feedback that you have veered off course.

When you are in alignment with your soul, you feel in a

state of flow where most things in your life just fall into place. You know that your soul is trying to get a message to you when things start to 'go wrong'. Although it's incredibly difficult when things 'go wrong' in your life, it's actually a message that something within yourself and your life needs attention. Your pain and the challenges you face can be your greatest teachers, if you are willing to listen to the messages they bring.

I would like to support you to get in alignment with your soul so that you can create the life that you truly desire and move beyond unhappiness and struggle.

Part of your purpose is to have a physical experience here upon this Earth, and part of your past experiences have come from your soul's desire to know pain, suffering and duality. But we have arrived at a time on our planet when it's possible to move beyond duality, to move beyond these old karmic patterns and become conscious creators upon this Earth.

I believe that you are a part of the great change happening on this planet. I believe that you have come to this planet with something magnificent to express. This is an energy that you share. *Your purpose* is to fully be you, imparting all that you are to others and the world. You will be guided to take action in life, but your purpose is more of a *being* than a doing. From your being, everything that you do, all action that you take, will be aligned with your *true essence*. This is your great purpose here upon this earth.

You have been shut off from your super powers, from the conscious awareness that you do make your own reality. It's now time to learn how to consciously create the life you want rather than unconsciously creating the life you don't want.

If this concept is new for you, I will ask you at this point to stay open to learning a new way of being, a new way of playing with your life. It's so much fun and incredibly empowering knowing that you can consciously refashion your life for the better.

Receive Money, Receiving You

The core of what we are doing here with money manifestation is learning how to deeply love and value yourself. Receiving money is the same as receiving you. There are lots of ways that money can show up in a person's life. This practice is about money manifestation in alignment with your soul, in alignment with your higher self.

I have noticed that through the practice of money manifestation, something much more profound also happens, which I believe is why this journey is so important. Money manifestation in alignment with your soul's purpose is the deeper practice of learning to receive all of you, to fully love yourself and value yourself.

Money manifestation is about connecting to your soul, to the truth of who you are. This money manifestation mastery practice is also about connecting to your soul's purpose. What are you here to experience? Why did you decide to come here? What are you here to share with the world? Who are you? Money manifestation is about clearing the path to your truth and your purpose.

This process is about stepping into who you are and sharing your greatness with the world. This is about sharing your gifts, the gift of who you are, just by being here, present upon this Earth.

Manifesting the Life You Desire

You are the creator of your life. You get to choose. If you don't like what's showing up, change it. Much of your life is determined by the unconscious thoughts, beliefs and emotions that are dictating your decisions and actions, something of which you are unaware. What you want to do and what we are working towards here is consciously designing your life, rather than unconsciously creating a life based on your inner blocks.

What works best and creates the greatest flow is when you create your life in alignment with your higher self, your soul, your being. Your higher self is also involved in this process.

You have come here to learn and experience in accordance with a specific design. Consciously aligning with your higher self brings in the good intended for your life. This doesn't mean that life will be easy, but finding alignment with your soul will allow greater ease for you.

Money manifestation at its best is when you are manifesting your true nature, living in your purpose. You can bring about what you want from the level of the ego, but this usually does not result in positive benefits. Living your life driven by your ego or personality self will often only bring more drama, emotional highs and lows, pain and suffering for you and for those around you.

If you are not enjoying an aspect of your life, this is a sign, a message from your higher self, that something within yourself or your life needs adjustment. This can mean an internal shift or an external shift. Everything starts within. Begin by shifting your internal world and your external world will be transformed for the better. You do not have to stay in struggle or in lack anymore.

If things are not showing up for you in the way that you

would like, you need to ask some questions and get some support. The trick is remembering to ask, remembering that you can choose a different reality for yourself. It's easy to get sucked into a seductive negative spiral. When that happens you can make the choice to change that negative mindset in the moment.

Ask yourself, 'What am I really asking for here? What would I like to show up here? What would I like my financial reality to be?' And then start asking for that to appear. Open up to the positive of what you truly want. It's easy to get lulled into what's not working and fall into negative creation. Most people have not been taught how to consciously create the life that they want. We have learned from the model whereby people moan and complain when dissatisfied with life.

You have been shown misery, you have been shown suffering and victimhood. You have not been shown that it's possible to redirect your life.

So what do you wish to experience? As we are focusing on money, what do you want as your financial reality?

Creating Your Magical Life

Receiving is about re-connecting to your ability to create magic. Money manifestation is like playing with magic, which is why it's so much fun. Let's see what you can manifest. It's playtime!

Money manifestation, receiving money, is about tapping into you, your magic, your gifts, your wisdom, everything you've come here to share, everything you've come here to experience.

Your Super Powers

You have forgotten your super powers; you have forgotten how strong and transcendent you truly are. The deeper purpose of this book is to 'Activate Your Power', while we 'Activate Your Abundance'. We are activating your truth, your purpose, and ultimately activating who you truly are. You are not the little good-for-nothing human that you have been pretending to be, far from it.

It is radical for a conscious, heart centred being to welcome money into your life in the way that we are speaking about in this book. In our society, as we currently know it, there has been an unconscious message that you are not allowed to be that powerful, that you are not allowed to be too great or too spectacular. Most of society is set up to keep you small, to keep you limited, to keep you shut down, to keep you disempowered and separated from others. Then everyone around you conspires to keep this principle in place, especially family and friends.

No one has taught you to be great. Perhaps no one has told you who you truly are and how extraordinary you are. If you have never been told how amazing you are, now is the time to hear this message.

Dear one, you are a magnificent being. There is no one else like you in the entire Universe. You are unique and you are very special. Your brilliance is needed here. You are here to share your genius with us for a reason. Welcome. You have full permission to shine.

Are you ready to Activate your awesome, magical, powerful, happy, wealthy being? If so, read on my friend. This is going to be fun.

What Happens When You Block Receiving?

It's impossible to disconnect yourself from source energy. You are part of the Universe and always connected to it, but you can block yourself from this connection. It's like the flow of a river that is stopped by a dam. You can block yourself from receiving the energy that is there for you, but it does not go away.

When you stop yourself from receiving, this takes you out of flow with your life and out of alignment with yourself. When you block receiving you are turning your back on source energy, from Universal flow, from your being, from your soul. When you are doing this, it's not conscious, so please don't condemn yourself. But on some level not accepting what is yours is a rejection of your true nature, a rejection of life and a rejection of what is truly possible for your life upon this Earth.

These are some of the symptoms you can experience when not receiving what is your true self:

- Stress
- Tension
- Exhaustion
- Anxiety
- Depression
- Sadness
- Feeling alone
- Lost
- Confused
- Doubt
- Shame
- Guilt
- Financial Lack
- Working hard for money
- Feeling undeserving
- Feeling not good enough

When you are in flow with Universal energy and your higher self you will feel more:

- ❖ Connected
- ❖ In Flow
- ❖ Aligned
- ❖ Purposeful
- ❖ Fulfilled
- ❖ Happy
- ❖ Joyful
- ❖ Energised
- ❖ Focused
- ❖ Clear
- ❖ Peaceful
- ❖ Abundant

What would you prefer to experience?

No Longer a Victim

It's time to let go of victim consciousness. No more feelings of powerlessness, no more blaming and pointing the finger when things don't go your way. As my dad always said to me: *'When you point your finger, there are always three fingers pointing back at you.'* If you are going to change your financial reality for the better, if you are going to change your life for the better, you need to take full responsibility for how your life is now and from this point onwards.

Humans don't like to take responsibility for their lives. In a moment of pain and disappointment it is so much easier to blame. This way you don't have to look at the part that you play in how your life is turning out. But the truth is, being a victim is a much more painful way of living. Being a victim compromises your ability to do anything about the direction of your life.

There may have been truly awful things that happened to you on your journey. I am so sorry for any suffering you have endured. I truly am. Any harm inflicted on you is a part of your life story. You can never erase your past. You can't change the past, but you can change your response to your past and any decisions that you made based on your past experiences. You have the power to determine how you feel about life. You have the power to determine your response to life and your thoughts and beliefs about life, which is a transformative, empowering, life-affirming ability.

Most of your pain and suffering comes through the mind and emotions. The good news is your mind and emotions are subject to your control. You have the ability to change your life, your perspective on your past and your future.

You can choose to be a victim of your past, a victim of your life, or you can choose to consciously alter how you think and feel now to make a different future for yourself. It's your choice.

For the Love of Money

Have you heard of the saying, 'Whatever you focus on grows'? Well, it's true, whatever you focus on—*consistently*—grows. This is true whether it's *good* or *bad*. One of the problems that I see with heart centred people is that they have ignored, rejected and neglected money.

You may consider financial money matters to be unimportant, pretend money doesn't exist, judge it, refuse it, reject it, and even hate it. Or you may have made making money very hard work and no fun at all. No wonder things have not been working out so well.

Ideally, you need to learn to love money. Loving it means honouring it, valuing it and treating it with care. If you can't love money, at least be willing to bring your attention to it. From having an awareness of it, you can then grow to an acknowledgment of it, to appreciating money, honouring money and perhaps eventually, expand into loving money. Up until now money has been partially neglected, and anything that is neglected won't thrive, whether that's a relationship, your health, your garden, your house, or anything else in life.

From this level of money manifestation and abundance, learning to love money is about learning to love yourself. Your relationship with wealth is an extension of your relationship with yourself, your relationship with the world and life itself.

Much of how you interact with finances is learned behaviour handed down to you, so now you are going to begin the journey of healing your relationship with money, healing your relationship with yourself, healing your relationship with life and start a building a new life towards financial freedom.

Money Manifestation

Now it's time to play with magic! This is my favourite subject and you don't even need a magic wand! You can get yourself a magic wand if that makes it seem more realistic, but it's not necessary :)

Manifestation is your ability to ask for what you want and then be open to receiving it. It's so much easier than you think! The challenge is to get out of your own way. When you are no longer standing in the way, everything good can flow in.

How Do You Receive?

'Step 2: Release' prepares you for 'Step 3: Receive'. Releasing your money blocks and barriers opens you up to the process of receiving. You will now be guided through the steps to receiving.

The Power Behind Your Intention

It's time to get crystal clear on your intention. I say intention because you want to stay open to how this shows up. The ego, the personality self, can become fixated on the specifics of appearances. Your ego and mind have a very limited perspective on what is possible for you and your life. Your mind can only understand what it already has experienced. There are infinite possibilities to how your dreams can show up for you that you may not even know exist yet.

It's fine for you to ask for details but there is a benefit in staying receptive to how things will show up. One way to accept however wealth manifests physically for you is by connecting to the feeling behind what you want. What are you really asking for?

Let's say someone wants a red sports car. What is that person really asking for? Is it just the red sports car or is it the *feeling* that the red sports car gives them? How does that person want to *feel* when they're behind the wheel of this dream car? I imagine that they are seeking a feeling of freedom and excitement, maybe a sense of power and sexiness. Ultimately this person longs for a *feeling* through the red sports car.

Manifestation is most effective when you connect to the feeling of what you are asking for. What do you want to feel via your money goal? Manifestation is not really about the thing that you desire itself, it's not about money just for the sake of money. Money is a vehicle to experience what you most wish to have.

If you are asking to experience freedom, power, excitement and sexuality, with the red sports car example, there are lots of ways that these feelings can show up for you. Yes, you can ask for that car, that's exciting, but you really want to connect to what your soul is asking to experience. Your higher self does not care about a tangible object in itself, but is instead seeking an experience, a feeling that can be found through the vehicle of the sports car.

The Universe wants to gift you many wonderful ways in which you can express these intangible desires, so stay open to receiving all of the infinite possibilities. Yes, you can have a sports car, absolutely, but there may be even better ways that you can experience freedom, excitement, power and sexuality that you don't know about yet.

Ask for what you want but be willing to accept what other possibilities can manifest in your life.

This process is not about fixating on the object itself, although do include specifics. The thing that you desire is not going to make you happy ultimately. You may get a momentary joy, but physical things alone won't sustain your emotional wellbeing forever.

The most important piece is connecting to the WHY, the WHY behind your intention. Those feelings of freedom, excitement, power and sexuality can show up in your life in many ways. Open up to the infinite realm of what is available to you while asking for the physical manifestation of money or what it can buy.

To be clear, yes, ask for what you want, money or the red sports car, but make sure you know why you really want it. What's it for? What are you really hoping to experience through the vehicle of that physical item. Your WHY will give you the fuel you need to manifest your desires and will ultimately lead you to be happier in your life as your answers begin to appear. Physical items won't ultimately fulfil you, it's your inner state of being that will. But through the physical, you can experience the miraculous practice of bringing your heart and soul to the material world.

Holding the Vision

Let's say it's a car that you want. Get clear on your vision. You want to see it in your mind's eye. You want to imagine yourself in it. What would driving it feel like? How does the car physically feel? Bring up those feelings in your body now. What would it smell like? What would it sound like?

For manifestation to work best, you need to bring your goals into all of your senses. See, feel, hear, touch, and taste what you seek. You want to imagine the car as if it's real, as if it's here right now in your present reality.

Now connect to your 'Money Goal'. See yourself with that money as if it's yours now. Feel what it would be like to have that money, see what it would look like to have that money. How would you walk or talk with this money? How would you dress, what would you do, how would you act with this money? Bring your financial goal into what can be known by all of your senses. Don't keep your goal in the future. Imagine that it is happening now. Become it now.

Include your money WHY in this visualisation exercise. Bring up the feeling of what you truly desire. If it's a feeling such as freedom that your money goal would provide, what does freedom feel like, taste like, smell like, look like?

You may be more attuned to one of your senses more than the others. You may be more visual or you may be more tactile, for example. Try to incorporate all of your senses into this exercise. It feels good and can be fun too.

As you bring your intentions into the moment as if it exists now, you are coming into vibrational alignment with what you are asking for now. Therefore, the feeling of what you want is in existence now. Do you see? You are creating your reality in those few seconds that you are envisioning your dreams.

If what you are asking for is freedom, you can choose to feel freedom right now. Therefore, you have instantly manifested what you long to have. It is yours now. As you practice connecting to the feeling, you will allow this feeling to be part of your day-to-day life. It's like training a new muscle. Here you are training the freedom muscle. As you strengthen your senses every day, you will welcome more of what you want into your life.

Most often you unconsciously push what you want away or keep what you desire at bay. This is a fascinating part of being human. You may say you want freedom, joy, love, health and wealth, but are you willing to let this into your reality? If you have not fully experienced what you are asking for in this life, part of you will have no idea what it is to have that love, joy, peace or wealth. It may be a new experience for you to have this. Your protective ego self can therefore flare up when you start moving towards what you want as these 'positive' states of being can feel like a threat. If you are asking for true love but have only experienced being rejected in your past, then love can feel like a threat and your protective walls can go up when love comes near. This means that you end up pushing away the very thing that you are asking for. It sounds crazy but this is what every human being does to one degree or another.

Begin training yourself to be willing to receive what you are hoping for. You need to teach yourself that it's okay to welcome these amazing experiences into your life. As you consciously accept more of what you want into the present moment, you will be better equipped to take in the true gifts you are meant to have.

Vision Board

Look at your vision board every day as part of 'Step 3: Receive'. Hold the vision of what you want and step into your money goal and your new money mindset. This is a powerful practice, one that will create profound change in your life if you persist and continue with it.

Keep adding to your vision board as you move along on your money manifestation journey. You will have more that you ask for as you grow, evolve and expand. You may also discover new money blocks that you weren't aware of. Find the opposite of that money block and write it on your vision board.

I discovered that it was difficult for me to receive love on my money manifestation journey. I uncovered a core wound that believed I was alone and unsupported. This wound was pushing out the love, connection and wealth that I was truly wanting. On my vision board I wrote, 'Opening up to love', 'Welcoming love in', and, 'I am loved and supported'. I then began to visualise bringing love into my body. I practiced receiving love in. At first this was tough for me, because on some deep level I didn't know how to be genuinely loved. But the more I practiced it, the easier it became. Then my external reality started to express this inner shift. I started attracting more love, new friendships, as well as enjoying improved relationships with my kids and my husband. I still practice opening up to receive love most days, as it's a work in progress.

Study each item on your vision board, one at a time. Have the vision board in front of you to look at once you have learned 'Step 1: Relax' and 'Step 2: Release'. The function of the vision board is to remind you what you are asking for. It can become easy to forget your dreams and get caught up in what is not working.

Having your vision board is like knowing where you are going on the map. You don't necessarily know exactly what the journey is going to look like or be like. There may be twists and turns in the road, but when you are clear on your destination, even if you aren't certain exactly what the journey will be like or what the new place you are going to will be like, you will know where you are going and find your way there eventually.

Have your vision board with you when you start 'Step 1: Relax'. After Step 1 and 2 review your vision board. You now want to connect with what you are seeking. Read the words or look at the pictures. Bring what you are asking for into your senses. You want to see your dreams, feel them, smell them, hear them, taste them.

Some people I have worked with like to create a more beautiful vision board on Pinterest. You are welcome to do this but make sure that you can see it every day. I prefer the physical version of a vision board as you're likely to notice it at various points in the day. Choose whatever version works best for you.

Asking for Money

'Step 3: Receive' begins by asking for what you want. Ask this question every day as part of your daily 'Abundance Activation' practice.

'What would it take to bring in more than X amount of money every month/year with ease and joy? Anything and everything in the way of this, I let go of now.'

Who are you asking with this question? This depends on your belief system. From my perspective, you are asking the Universe, your higher self, your unconscious mind and your conscious self. It's a team effort! All these aspects of your life and who you are work together to help make your dreams come true.

Next you want to connect to your money WHY, your money fuel. Consider each item and say:

'What would it take to feel…?'

'What would it take to have…?'

'What would it take to (do, experience)…?'

Fill in the gaps to adjust to your specific request, then

add the releasing statement:

'Anything in the way of this showing up with ease, I let it go now.'

As you allow yourself to receive, your money blocks will also come up. You will be both receiving and releasing as you activate this process. Be aware of the thoughts, feelings and emotions that appear which are not in alignment with what you truly want. Keep releasing as you open up to receive.

Vibrational Alignment

Vibrational alignment is a practice of bringing what you're asking for into the present moment as if it exists NOW. This is how you make The Law of Attraction work for you. By becoming that which you desire, by bringing what you want into your body in the NOW, you are attracting it into your life, drawing that experience you are in pursuit of towards you now. You are becoming what you are hoping for now. You are becoming the vibration of what you desire.

Most people say, 'I will feel free when...' 'I will allow myself space to rest when ....' 'I will be happy when...' 'I will be joyful when this happens, when that happens.' But what you want to do is bring what you want in the NOW, and become it now, rather than waiting for some outside circumstance to make it happen. You must make tangible that which you hope for in the present, otherwise your dreams will always remain in the future.

You have the power to choose how you are feeling right now. It's not always easy to shift how you are feeling. It takes effort, but you are able to choose what you really want now. For example, if you are asking for freedom, you can choose to feel freedom right now. Freedom is a choice in this moment. To become in vibrational alignment with freedom all you need to do is ask.

Exercise:

Close your eyes, breathe and feel into your body. Ask for your body to become the vibration of freedom now and be aware of how it feels. Try this now.

Let's look at the vibration of joy, for example. Bring the feeling of joy into your body now. Become the vibration. It may take a few moments to sift through any heavy energy within to feel it, so be patient, ask, breathe and wait.

How does that feel? How does freedom feel? How does joy feel? The more you consciously become what you want now, the more you will attract that very thing to you. How cool is that? You become a magnet for what you want by becoming what you want *vibrationally* now. When you vibrate what you want, you allow what you want to physically manifest in reality in the present moment.

I'd like you to think about your big WOW goal. What is that amount? Imagine yourself having that money now. How does it feel to possess that much? If you had that wealth in your life now, how would you walk? How would you talk? How would you act in the world? How would you feel? See yourself with this money now. What is the vibration? Close your eyes and take a breath. How does that feel in your body? What is the energy of that in your body? How does that become palpable?

Practice stepping into this vibration as often as possible. You become what you are asking for every day. Act on this once a day as a minimum.

The Law of Attraction works as you allow yourself to become the vibration of what you want NOW; you draw what you want towards you into your reality. You become a magnet for that abundance to show up physically for you in real time.

As you start stepping into this new truth of money and wealth, you are practicing the art of bringing money and wealth into your reality. You are reprogramming yourself to be able to accept what you are longing for into your life now.

By becoming the vibration of what you want, you are releasing the money blocks that are not in alignment with what you're requesting. You are creating your situation all the time. You end up attracting into your reality whatever you are vibrating.

You are the creator of your life. What are you vibrating now? If you aren't enjoying it, change it.

Exercise: Stepping Into Money

Connect back to your money goal. For this exercise write your 'Money Goal' on a piece of paper and put it on the floor a foot in front of you. Take a moment and stand where you are now and feel into your body. Take a few deep breaths. Now I would like you to step onto that piece of paper, onto that amount that you would like to receive. Now imagine yourself with that sum of money. Embody it. Possess it! What does it feel like to have that much wealth? What are the sensations in your body? Stand there for a few minutes breathing into that new abundance.

This is a practice of *becoming* money. This is allowing yourself to receive that amount of money. Do this every day to get more comfortable with allowing this financial reality into your life. This is training for the goal to become real. It's another powerful money manifestation tool.

Now try it with your big WOW amount. How does that feel in your body?! Practice playing with both amounts each day. Start with your first step intention and then move up to your WOW amount.

Personally, I love playing with the WOW goal. This makes my body the most excited and happy. This is the amount that will stretch you furthest.

Once you get the hang of this exercise, you don't need to stand on the piece of paper. You can do this sitting in your 'Relax' position.

Filling Your Golden Wealth Pot

When I first started writing this book a beautiful vision came to me. I was shown the image of a big golden pot in a cave. There was a stream of liquid gold flowing gracefully and consistently into the big golden pot. The liquid kept pouring in, the river of gold was continuously flowing. Once the golden pot was full, all the excess gold trickled out of the pot and went out into the world to be shared with the rest of humanity. The pot was always filled with gold, as there was a continuous stream of gold pouring into it. It was never drained or emptied. It was always full and there was plenty for everyone.

This pot of gold represents your inner being. Filling your pot is about making sure that you are always full, that your needs are met, that you are taken care of, that you are supported. Having a full pot means that you have what you need, that you are healthy, wealthy, always have enough energy, that you are satisfied. When your pot is full, when you have everything you need, then any excess energy, time or money you have can go out into the world around you to benefit others, and this generosity will never drain your pot.

Energetically this golden pot lives deep within your pelvis.

Many heart-centred, caring people drain their energy for the sake of others. When you give to everyone else first, without seeing to your own needs, the result is a lack of self-sufficiency. Giving energy out with nothing coming back is exhausting, it drains your life force and is an unsustainable way to live.

The truth is, when you are draining your energy for others, you are not really serving others or yourself because you are drawing from a place of lack.

How do you serve others best? When you are drained,

exhausted, depleted? Or do you serve best when your needs are met, when you have energy, when you feel whole and complete within? What awareness comes to you with this question?

Let's bring this back to money. When do you serve others best? When you are broke, in financial lack, with limited funds? Or do you serve best when all of your financial needs are met, when you have more than sufficient means? What awareness comes to you with this question?

I have spoken to many people who feel that if others are broke, starving and struggling, then it's wrong for them to have financial gain and every need met. They consider it greedy to have when others don't.

Question: *How can you make the greatest impact in the world? With money or without money?*

For me the answer is always 'with money'. If you had more money than you personally needed, what would you want to do with that excess?

This doesn't mean that you can't make an impact without money. Of course you can. But this idea that somehow it's righteous or better not to have money is a lie and an effective way to limit yourself in almost every avenue.

Whatever you choose as your reality is absolutely fine.

There is no right or wrong, no good or bad, but I hope to show you that it's more than okay to have your dreams realised. In fact, I believe that when you allow yourself to have, and stop limiting yourself in every area of your life, including money, so much more is possible. You can make a greater impact from this place of financial abundance.

Let's reframe this. The concept of the golden wealth pot is to visualise the benefit of valuing yourself, putting yourself first, knowing that when your pot is full, you will have more to give. There's more than enough to share when your needs and wants are fulfilled. No more depleting your resources to help others, no more holding yourself back so that others don't feel bad. No more limiting yourself because of what others might say or do. It's time to fill your pot.

I am shown this analogy over and over again when working with clients. When you board an airplane, the stewardess will tell you, In the event of emergency on an aeroplane we are told, 'When the oxygen mask drops down, place the mask over your own mouth and nose before assisting others.' Why is that? Why should you put your own oxygen mask on first? If you can breathe, then you can help others put their oxygen masks on and breathe. If you're concerned first with everyone else, you will run out of oxygen and pass out. You are limited in how many people you can support without oxygen.

The more you give to yourself, the more you can give to others.

There are lots of ways that you can express yourself with money. You have seen many ways of having money that don't resonate with you. We have seen the connection between money and greed, money and the abuse of power, money and separation, money and misery. You get to choose what you want for your relationship with money. I am inviting you into the possibility of seeing money manifestation as an act of deep self-love and empowerment. Welcoming money into your life is the practice of self-love.

What is the impact of loving yourself as you express that love in the world? What is the impact of knowing your true worth and valuing yourself on the world? What is the impact of your needs being met? What is the impact of your loving and valuing yourself as that love is reflected on those around you, your children, your family, your friends, your lover, on society? What is the impact of having more money in your life? What does that do? What does that allow? Please journal on this and see what comes into your awareness.

Exercise

Imagine a golden pot in your pelvis. There is a stream of liquid gold trickling in from the Universe, coming down onto the crown of your head, through your body, filling your golden wealth pot as it sits in your pelvis. Imagine this golden pot filling up to the brim. Once full, allow the liquid gold to spill over the edge, trickling out into the world around you.

How does this feel? What appears for you? Journal about this experience.

How Much are you Willing to Receive?

The Universe will gift you as much as you are willing to receive. How much are you willing to accept? How much happiness can you hold? How much joy can you experience? How much expansion will you allow? How much freedom…? How much abundance…? How much love? All of these states of being can feel intense if they are not familiar to you.

You can have an opening into receiving then quickly find the shutters close to bring you down again. How much do you block the good stuff in life because it's uncomfortable? Receiving all that life has to offer you can be intense.

This is why I recommend a daily practice where you keep stepping into your abundance so that you become accustomed to having more and more. It's a practice of expanding, a practice of opening your heart, a practice of letting the money in and accepting love.

Journal on this question or close your eyes and ask yourself:

'Where am I blocking myself from receiving?' See what comes to your awareness. Would you be willing to stop denying yourself and let all of life come in?

On a daily basis invite your energetic walls, barriers and protection from life to drop away. Breathe in all that is offered to you. It will prove to be wildly wonderful. This is where the money manifestation magic happens.

Having Money Vs. Spending Money

I used to think that the purpose of money was to spend it. I became very good at manifesting money but I was equally good at getting rid of money. I watched myself play this game of bringing in wealth and disposing of it again and again.

I then started exploring the difference between having money and spending money. I started to realise that I was uncomfortable allowing myself to *have* money. Having money was about allowing myself to accept it. Having money was about valuing myself enough to feel worthy of it.

I'd like you to explore in your money journal, what is the purpose of money? Bring your awareness to anywhere you might be devaluing or disposing of money.

I would like to invite you to practice filling up your wealth pot, to allow yourself to possess money. This is the practice of agreeing to have money, not from a state of greed, not from a state of desperation, not from a state of need, but allowing yourself to have money as an act of self-love.

This practice of having money, filling your wealth pot, is the act of stepping into the energy of the divine feminine. The divine feminine is your Queen energy, the energy of the Empress, the energy of the Goddess. And if you are a man reading this, step into the energy of the King.

What qualities does the Queen have? From my experience, the Queen lives in total abundance. There's no energy lack around her. The Queen has a full wealth pot, her needs are met, she never struggles, she's not in lack, she's not grasping onto things, her spirit is at peace and she holds the reins of her power. A Queen knows who she is and that she is provided for.

From the energy of the Queen, the Empress, the Goddess, the divine feminine energy, you draw all of life, including money, towards you. This is the practice of receiving.

Our society runs on an energy of trying, doing and forced action, which over time drains energy, especially for female bodies. The Goddess, the Empress, the Queen allows herself space to rest and be, because in that space of being, so much magic transpires. The Queen draws everything that she needs to her from this space of being. Now it's time for you to embody this as well. Step into your Queen energy.

10% Account

The 10% account is where you pay yourself first. You put 10% of all of your income into an account you never spend. This fund can then accumulate wealth over time. It's a place where your money can grow.

You can call your 10% account your 'Self-Love Account' or 'The Valuing You Account'. When you have ample funds in that account you begin feeling secure, safe, supported and cared for. You can begin to relax!

When I first started using my 10% account I would fill

it to a certain point and then I would drain it. I would spend all of the money I had saved. I spent my 10% account on things that were important to me, that I felt were valuable. But after I saved and then drained my 10% account a few times, I had to ask myself some big questions.

After some honest inquiry it became clear to me just how uncomfortable I was in allowing myself to have money. On a deeper level this was a discomfort with receiving, with feeling secure, supported and ultimately loved. My programming was set to keep me in a state of having then losing, in momentary peace then lack. This was created from pain in my past that was still unconsciously driving me.

With this awareness, I renewed my commitment to never spend my 10% account again. The 10% account for me is a way of practicing self-love, self-care, as well as feeling safe, supported and secure.

Every step of your money manifestation journey will reveal fascinating discoveries about yourself and your relationship with life. There are great opportunities for self-growth and empowerment on this path to 'Money Manifestation Mastery'.

On an energetic level money wants to grow, it wants to expand, it's a creative energy that needs nurturing. It doesn't want to stay stuck in a stagnant bank account not growing. That is stifling to the energy of money; money wants to increase. You can choose to invest the money in your 10% account anywhere your money will grow.

On a deeper level, your 10% account is about valuing yourself and loving yourself enough to have money. On this plane it's not even about money. But the idea of money, physical money, accumulating and working effortlessly for your good, allows your whole being to relax.

An interesting feature of money is that it's so easy to spend. It's so easy to get rid of money. As you gain more wealth, you will most likely increase your spending, leaving you no better off financially than before. Get into the habit now of paying yourself first, putting aside 10% of your income, every week or month, in an account that you never touch. This way your wealth pot can accelerate and expand. You can then educate yourself in ways to invest your money and help it grow.

The 10% account is a practice that will show up in all sorts of ways. Journal on your thoughts or feelings about the 10% account. What comes up for you?

You might like the idea of a 10% account but feel that you can't afford to do that now. If putting aside 10% each week or month simply feels impossible, start with 5%. If

5% is impossible for you, put 10% account on your vision board as an intention for the future. You can also put 'Wealth Pot' on your vision board to remind you to keep loving and nurturing this concept.

End of Chapter Actions

- Sign up for the book bonuses:
- http://larawaldman.com/money-manifestation-mastery-book-bonuses/
- Practice Step 1: Relax, Step 2: Release, Step 3: Receive daily
- Study your vision board after Step 2
- Breathe in money, love, your connection to the divine
- Step into vibrational alignment with your money goals
- Bring your WOW goal into the now, become it now
- Fill Your Golden Wealth Pot
- Keep releasing any blocks that you come up against
- How much money would you like in your wealth pot? Include this amount on your vision board
- Journal on Where are you pushing money away?
- Set up your 10% account

Chapter 5

Step 4: Rhythm

"You don't have a Soul, you are a Soul. You have a body."

– The Buddha

When I first started playing with manifestation, and for a long time after that, I was only using my first three steps to 'Abundance Activation', 'Relax', 'Release', and 'Receive'. These first 3 steps alone did work to a degree, but I realised a big piece was missing and that was 'Step 4: Rhythm'.

'Step 4: Rhythm' is the part of money manifestation that requires you to be physically present in your body, in your life on this planet and taking guided action from your intuition, higher self and the Universe. With Step 4 you are birthing, anchoring, everything you're asking for into the physical realm.

We are going to be looking at why this is challenging for many heart-centred beings and what might come up to stop you from being fully present in your body and in your life.

Step 4: Rhythm – Part 1
Manifestation through your Body

You can think about money all day long, you can visualise money all day long, you can pray and scream from the mountaintops for money to come into your life. On the other realms of consciousness, beyond this physical plane, all of this will work.

Money comes to you energetically the moment you ask for it. As you request money, it will be gathering in piles, in great mountains of energetic cash all around you, but it will end there. The energetics of money is different from the embodiment of money in our physical reality.

The first 3 steps we have covered will help you activate your abundance, call money in and welcome it, but if there is no physical vehicle for money to come through, money won't be able show up easily for you on the physical level.

What is Manifesting Money through your Body?

The first part of manifesting money through your body is about all of you, your soul, your higher self, your consciousness, being present in your physical body, in your physical life, here on earth. I find that the majority of people on the planet, especially sensitive souls, are not fully embodied. They are more like walking, talking heads, energetically shut off from the neck down or the waist down.

When I was a child I was completely off in La La land. People do call me La for short! My oldest friend tells the story of how I used to wander around the classroom, mid-lesson, daydreaming. I had no idea I was doing this. I was so deep in my daydream that I didn't even realise I was circling the classroom. I used to sleepwalk, bash into things and trip over myself a lot. I have four scars on my head from stitches as proof.

Why was I so ungrounded and out of sync with my body? In the other planes of existence where I was hanging out in dreamland, everything was bliss. I was in my happy place.

When you are present in your body, you feel everything. One protection method to avoid feeling is to check out and escape from your body. This means pulling your consciousness, your awareness out of your physical being.

The result of pulling out of the body for most adults is to be very busy in the mind. When you are fully embodied, fully present in your body, your mind will be more still. A busy mind means that you are not fully present in your body.

In order for money to show up in your life, *you* need to show up in your life. Most people are only half-aware in their life. Most people are like walking heads. All of their activity is in the mind and they are shut off from the body. When you ask for what you want, energetically it is there instantly, but money needs to come through a vehicle in physical form in order to be accessible in the world. This happens with greater speed when you participate in your physical life, in your body and in your business. Can you imagine how much more effective you would be in your life if you were fully here?

For me, showing up fully in my life, in my body, felt like going to my death. It was a terrifying prospect. I felt unsafe here on the planet amongst all the chaos, pain and wild human emotions. The only place I felt safe was in nature, with animals, or young children.

But in truth, being present more in my body, in my business and in my life has allowed me to experience the joys of living on this planet more fully. I was missing out on so many wonderful possibilities by checking out. We experience pleasure through our body. Your body is a great pleasure vehicle.

Manifestation through your body is about you being fully embodied, *you* fully showing up in your physical state on this planet. Many of the tools we have been playing with in these teachings have been very energetic. Now we want to anchor all of those energetic practices so that this money (and anything else that you want to manifest) can show up here in the physical realm. Otherwise, it's all etheric, it's all out there, floating around in the ether.

The goal is to bring everything that you are seeking into the physical world and that is done through the vehicle of your body, in the form of your business, through assets, through investments and sometimes through other peoples' bodies. For example, other people might give you money. Here you are opening up to receive money through a variety of physical means, but please don't wait around for someone's generosity. Take action and make it happen! By all means be open to receiving from anyone who wishes to gift it to you, but don't let other people be your only source of wealth.

On a deeper level, becoming fully embodied is about your soul coming onto this planet, into your body, making the most out of your physical experience here on Earth.

Embodiment is about you acknowledging who you are, sharing the gift of you, sharing your light, sharing your wisdom. Embodiment is also about having a really cool and awesome physical expression, birthing ideas into reality, taking concepts, ideas, inspirations and making them become something physical. This is pure creation. It's time to fully arrive here in your body on this planet so that you can manifest what you are hoping and dreaming for.

What Happens when you are not Fully Embodied

It is hard to manifest the full potential of what you desire when you are not fully embodied. When you are ungrounded, you can still move and function in your life to a certain degree but part of your being is not here. Part of you is hovering above your everyday activities. From this ungrounded place, you will not find it easy to make the full impact you are destined to bring about.

It is hard to take consistent action when you are not fully embodied. You might have lots of ideas, big visions, big dreams, but taking those concepts and putting them into action can be challenging if you are not present in your physical body. Taking action when you are not embodied is like trying to drive a car from the back seat and saying, *'Car, why aren't you driving? Why aren't you moving? Why isn't this working?'* In some cases, it's similar to not even being in the car and wondering why won't it work. To drive a car, you need to open the door, sit in the driver's seat, turn the engine on and put your foot on the gas. Some people are behind the wheel of the car, putting their foot on the gas but at the same time putting their foot on the brake pedal. It is very difficult to move when you are trying to accelerate and brake at the same time.

It's pretty clear what we have to do in order to drive a car. It's similar when taking action in your body and manifesting through the physical.

What Stops you from being Fully Embodied?

Fear stops you. Fear of not feeling safe, fear of being seen, fear of judgement, fear of being too much. Maybe you're too different. A lot of people that I speak to feel they are weird. Maybe you feel that somehow you are not allowed to be yourself. Maybe you feel there is no place for you here, that you don't fit in. As you go through life you learn to hide parts of yourself that don't conform.

Maybe you feel that there is something fundamentally wrong with you. I once held this belief and many people that I speak to feel the same way. When you believe that something is not right about you, this causes you to deny the truth of who you are.

If people around you aren't showing up fully, they can then squash others from being who they are and suppress others' truth. *'If I am not allowed to express the truth of me, then you aren't either.'* The message is: *'I'm not allowed to be me.'*

My greatest fear was the fear of attack, of ridicule, of persecution. This was a continuing battle I fought in my journey. I had an intense aversion to speaking out and sharing my truth. This fear stopped me from showing up fully in my life and my business.

If you are sensitive, it can be frightening being present in your body because you feel everything deeply, you feel the emotions of those around you, you feel the energies of the earth and society, you feel the intensity and density of life. This can be painful, so unconsciously, you withdraw from life, you pull out of your physical body.

Withdrawing is a form of protection that you have devised to manage your life. Pulling out of the body is an unconscious act. It's not a conscious choice to leave your body, it's more of a default reaction to protect yourself. When you leave the body you hang out on the etheric level where it's all love, light and peace, where you can play with the angels and the unicorns and the fairies. It feels good there!

You chose to be here in this body, on this planet, at this time. If you decided to be here, and as you are here now anyhow, why not make the most of it? I know it's intense,

I know it can be really uncomfortable at times, but the only way you can receive all that's meant for you from this physical experience is by fully showing up.

The majority of people on this planet have shut down and are disconnected from themselves, others and life itself. Because of this there is a strong temptation to disengage from your own body if the people around you aren't participating in the full energy of their body.

This is a powerful and necessary practice, to keep coming back to your body. Being embodied is not the way that most people do life on this planet. It's quite radical. We are trying to do life in a different way by connecting back to your true nature.

With embodiment you are sharing your essence with all life around you. You are coming back to you, you are coming home and by doing that you share your truth, your light with the earth, humanity and all life on this planet. This is enlightening for you and for everyone around you, your family, your ancestors, for society and future generations to come.

It's Time to Come out of Hiding

It is time to come out, my lovely. It's time to be yourself, in your body on this planet. When you do this, you are sharing the truth of who you are. By sharing who you are, you are sharing your light, your gifts, your wisdom, your uniqueness, the difference that you are here to make in the world.

Coming out of hiding is you stepping into your power. It's powerful sharing all that you are. You are a magnificent being. This embodiment process is about recognising that and reminding yourself of who you are each and every day. No more shrinking back, no more hiding.

When there are parts of you that you judge to be bad, ugly or not good enough, these are what you hide in the shadows. You want to bring all of you to the table, out into the light and let it all be seen. Once you bring these parts out, they are no longer in the dark, and you can finally tap into the gift behind these traits you deem not good enough, unacceptable, and unlovable.

I had a lot of anger as a child and as a teenager. As a young person, I was incredibly self-destructive and I turned this energy against myself. This rage within me manifested as dark and shadowy, which turned into drug use, eating disorders, depression and candida. But underneath it was a strong energy, a transformational energy, an energy that had the ability to heal. These gifts were hiding. I simply did not know any other way to manage my energy. I didn't know what to do with this power within me. This force within me couldn't handle the lies, the pain, the stagnant energy on this planet and wanted to shift and change it. It is now my practice to channel this energy within me and share it with the world, for good rather than to destroy myself.

Whatever judgements you have about yourself, there is gold hiding somewhere within. The hidden parts of you need to come out of the shadows and express themselves in their own unique authentic way. Your abilities are just beneath your pain.

Perhaps you were never fully received, never really seen for who you are. This is what happened for me. It was almost like I hadn't been given permission to be here. I didn't know how to show up here on the planet because no one had taught me how or given me permission. No one told me that it was okay to be me. You need to be received to be valued, as you do that you feel safe. We are now going to give you that permission to fully be you here, finally.

Part of the process of coming out and showing up in the truth of who you are is taking a look at where you shrink away. Spend some time journaling on the hidden parts of your life. Then continue to observe yourself in different situations and become aware of how you act in those situations. Do you shine your light? Do you share your truth? Or do you conceal who you are?

Calling on All of You to be Here Now

You are now going to make a commitment to fully be here and call on all of you to be in the now. This is a practice that I recommend doing on a daily basis, throughout the day. It is normal to energetically pull out of your body, to disconnect, so this is a practice to reel you back in every time you check out.

I would like to welcome all of you here. I welcome you to be in the world now. We are calling on all parts of you, all fragments, anything you have cut off from yourself, to be here now.

A long time ago, you made a decision that there were abilities you possessed that were unacceptable, facets that could not be seen. You banished these parts and hid them away, so far away that you may not even know they exist. You judged these to be dark, bad, ugly and unlovable.

You also learned to hide your beauty, your magic, your greatness, your great power that others couldn't handle. People in your life may have been threatened or triggered by your gifts, so you learned to push them away so as to be loved, received and to keep the peace. You hid what you judged to be 'bad' but you also hid what would be considered 'good'.

Through my years of working as a Healer, I have often met clients who've had all sorts of awful things happen to them in their life. The pain from these challenging life experiences was still carried in their body and energy field. This unresolved pain gets buried within the parts of you that you have locked away from this lifetime but pain can also be from other lifetimes as well. It doesn't matter if you believe in past lives, but it may be helpful for you to realise that there are beliefs and wounds that may not be from this incarnation. Your pain is not all from you. You can also take on family, ancestral or cultural trauma that has been handed down to you. It gets energetically passed down to you through your DNA.

I was given the awareness during a past life healing that I denied myself positive things in this life because I did some really terrible things in my past lives. Somewhere in that lifetime I made a vow that I'd never allow myself pleasure again. On some level I decided that I didn't deserve to receive because I had been so bad. I was punishing myself for all eternity. There were other lifetimes where I was trying to bring my light to the planet to create positive change and I was destroyed by this, I had been killed for doing this. So unconsciously I decided that it was unsafe to share the brightness of my spirit, and I locked it away.

You don't need to understand where your pain comes from or why you hide parts of yourself to do this portion of the 'Abundance Activation' process. All you need to be willing to do is to come back home, home to you.

This step in the 'Abundance Activation' process is about unlocking anything you have hidden. It's about bringing yourself out of hiding and calling all of you back in. I'd like to invite you to welcome yourself back home, come back to you.

We need all of you here now. You don't need to punish yourself for all eternity anymore. Have you not struggled enough already? Would you be willing to stop that now? You have permission. You can continue to punish yourself if you want, it's a choice, but you can also choose to forgive yourself, to forgive others, love all parts of you and move on. The past is the past. Now it's time to look forward and create a wonderful future for yourself, your family, friends and future generations.

Say the following statement every day to help yourself show up, to be present in your body and in your life. The words are not the most important part here, it's the intention behind the words. Feel free to change the wording in a way that resonates with you.

'I call on all of me to be here now. I call on all parts of me that I have cut off and hidden away to be here now. I welcome all of me here now, in this body, on this planet. I welcome myself home to me. I commit to being fully here in my body and in my life. Everything I've been shrinking away from, I let go of now. I expand into the truth of who I am and express the fullness of my being now. I share my light and my truth with myself and the world.'

Please know that coming into your body is a practice. Keep calling on yourself to be here and you will grow more and more comfortable staying here over time.

I have a daily practice of calling on all of me to be here now as I still pull out. Disconnecting is so unconscious. This is why you need to consciously remind yourself to be here as often as possible.

Karina's Story

The idea of creating an intuitive business programme had been floating around in my mind for a while but it wasn't until I started working with Lara that it all fell into place. As I was aligning with the vibration of my money goal I could feel my energy and inner power rising. I could see how my purpose was so closely linked to reaching a bigger tribe and working in an even deeper way than before.

I kept doing the 'Abundance Activation' inner work Lara invited us to do and one day the whole idea for the program became completely clear. I mapped it out and when I had to decide on the price I let the vibration of my income goal guide me.

This intuitive business programme ended up being at a higher price point than any of my other offers and it felt completely aligned to make it a 6-month long programme. I know that inner work and deep transformation take time and it felt amazing to finally own that, both for my clients and for myself.

During the creation and promotion time for my new programme, I kept doing the inner work and I could feel any money issues melt away and be replaced by a deeper sense of purpose and power.

I realised that underneath the money stories and challenges I was hiding my own light and that it was time to step up and become the true leader of my life.

This programme is now out in the world and it has been a true blessing to hold space for the most amazing women and watch them embrace their lives and soul's work with so much courage and love. It's also been very liberating to receive consistent income over 6 months and this has given me time to create other offers and to take even better care of myself.

Lara's techniques have helped me release old patterns and fears so that I could raise my energy and become the person who could hold space for this programme. I use her techniques daily and the results have been absolutely amazing – both financially and in my life. I am so grateful for this deep, inner work and for having met the amazing soul that is Lara.

Karina Ladet
Intuitive Channel, Healer & Mentor
www.karinaladet.com

Let's Get Into Your Body
Money Movement

So how do you get into your body? There are many delicious ways to achieve embodiment. One effective method is to move! Using your intuition, ask your body how it would like to move. *'Body, how would you like to move today? Would you like to dance, swim, walk, run, do yoga? How would your body like to play?'* Then, listen to the answers that pop into your awareness.

It's important to move every day to help you get into the physical. One of the ways that money comes to you is through your body. It is the vehicle to your physical experience here on this planet and also one of the means to welcoming money into your life.

There are many different ways that money can show up physically in your life, but it requires a vessel. You start with your physical form and then expand on to other ways. The foundation to this step is you being here, and from this strong, centred foundation, you can move on to create other places for money to land into the world such as business, assets or other people who want to give you financial gain.

A Playful Exercise

When you are moving your body, imagine bringing your big WOW money vision into your limbs through your movement. You are birthing that money into your life through your body while you move. Dance that money in, stretch that money in, run that money in. Do the same when you are making love. Birth that abundance through your body. If you don't have anyone to make love with, make love to yourself. Welcome wealth into your body through your pleasure. Let that money love flow in.

If you are feeling uncomfortable about this now, if things are stirring inside, get your money journal out and put those feelings down on paper. What thoughts, emotions or beliefs are surfacing for you? Get it out and mop it out. These are the energies that have been holding you back, keeping you stuck and small for too long now.

The patterns that stop wealth from coming into your life can be deeply engrained. Through the practice of 'Abundance Activation' and 'Money Manifestation Mastery', you are digging in areas that have been shut down for a long time. It's time for those false beliefs to be cleared now, to set yourself and your ancestors free once and for all.

This work is bigger than you. Making these shifts within will have a great impact on all life around you. You send ripples out in the Earth, society and the Universe, to create positive change. As you shift within you shift without. And here you thought this was just about making more money. No, my friend, this is about diving into who you truly are, your purpose, your magnificence and experiencing this extraordinary physical existence on this planet to the fullest.

Let's get into your body. You want to create a safe place for your being, your higher self, to land, for you to show up. Introducing… your amazing body!

Your physical self might not feel so comfortable at the moment. When you are carrying judgements, pain and trapped emotional energy, it can be uncomfortable. This is why it's critical to keep releasing, because when you free up the heavy stuff that no longer serves you, it feels a whole lot better being in your body.

Bodies like to move. Movement is one very practical way to get more into your body. Most often we like to move every day. Some days your body might really need to rest, in some moments your body might be asking to stop completely. But for the most part, bodies really like action.

I used to exercise like a maniac, pushing myself to work out hard five days a week. This way of exercising is not the kind of movement that I am speaking about here. I am not advocating for you to force yourself to exercise. I'm talking about listening to your body. *'Body, how do you want to move today?'* Your body will speak to you, your body will tell you what it needs. If you don't listen, it will begin to shout a little louder. If you ignore that, it will make you stop, which is what illness is often about. Your body is giving you signs and messages constantly. It's time to start listening to make greater harmony and improved function within your body. This will help you to enjoy your life more.

I'd like to invite you to move with the intention of coming into your body. Use your physical abilities mindfully and intentionally, calling all of you into your body, as a conscious present movement.

Your mind will wander when you withdraw from your body, and when you notice this happening, rein yourself back in. You want to be active in a way that profits your body. Be focused when in motion. Really feel your body.

I Love You, Body

How do you feel about your body? If you have a lot of judgements about your body, you will feel uncomfortable being in it. Judgements don't feel good. This is something that I struggled with for years. I had eating disorders; I hated my body, and felt disgusting, really disgusting. I was carrying so much pain in my poor little body and I just didn't know what to do about it.

You need to reconnect with your body, be united with your body. Then acknowledge all of those judgements that you are carrying. Talk to your body. What does it need? Imagine if you spoke to an animal or a child in the way that you speak to yourself. How abusive would that be?! Or imagine if you neglected a child or animal in the way that you neglect your body. What would that create?

Your body needs your love, your focus and attention, just like a child or an animal does. It needs your presence, your care. Talk to your body...

'What do you need, body? I am so sorry, please forgive me for all the cruel things I have said about you, for all of the ways that I have treated you badly. I'm so sorry, I love you.'

Our bodies, like young children and animals, are eager to forget harsh treatment and respond with forgiveness. Your body will happily release the pain it's held inside. Your body is here to serve you.

Body Gratitude

You cannot be here without your body so let's take a moment to appreciate it. Your body is your vehicle to experience this physical reality, so let's have a moment of gratitude for its service, yes?

Saying, 'I love you, body', might be a bit of a leap from how you relate to your body right now. You might not be able to love your body yet but you can start with body awareness. Would you be willing to bring your awareness to the physical form of all that you are?

Bringing your awareness to your body is very powerful. Your awareness is like a light in the dark places within. As you bring your light, anything that your body is feeling that does not work for you can begin to relinquish its hold on you.

After awareness, the next step is appreciating your body, appreciating all its good qualities.

'Hello, body. Thank you, body.'

Despite whatever is going wrong in your body, there are thousands of things that are very right in your body. It's incredible how we don't appreciate what works well until something breaks down. It's like the windshield wipers in a car. They don't seem that important until it pours with rain! It's not until you hurt a tiny part of your body that you realise what a big impact that member of your body has. Just take a moment to appreciate your body. Say…

'Thank you so much for all that you do, body.'

Could you love this body? That might be a work in progress, but it's what we want to arrive at, real love and appreciation for this body that you are in.

Body Touch

As well as saying *'I Love You, body'*, you can communicate to your body through touch. Bodies love touch, bodies need to be touched. Touch yourself lovingly every day. Why don't you try doing this right now? Stroke your legs, stroke your arms and your chest and your neck and your belly. Everything is interconnected, and as you are showing love to your body, this is also the practice of loving yourself.

When I was deeply bound by my body self-hate, I started to say, *'I love you. You're so beautiful.'* At first it felt like I was lying to myself. I didn't believe what I was saying. Then, to something I judged to be negative about my body, I would say, *'I love you, fat or cellulite.'* What I found amazing is that by simply giving your body love you can change the body. With love, excess fat can melt away, you can drop excess weight, you can reduce cellulite, you can look younger, simply by practicing self-love. Self-love is the ultimate Healer and perhaps the fountain of youth! Self-love is the key to health, happiness and vibrancy. Self-love makes you glow!

You are an Energetic Sponge

Our bodies are like big sponges. Much of the pain and suffering you experience in your body is energetic debris that you have picked up from the world around you, including judgements. All of the heaviness in your body is often pain, negative emotions, thoughts, beliefs, judgements and stuck energy. These energies often don't even belong to you! You are absorbing the energies of all life around you, your family, friends, work, society as well as your ancestors and cultural background. Would you be willing to let it all go?

When you love and appreciate your body, it gives your body permission to release anything that you don't need anymore. Your love, your attention, your appreciation, your loving touch will be giving your body permission to surrender anything that's stopping you from enjoying being in this body.

Humans respond to love. How well do you respond to criticism? You can witness this with children. How are you going to get the best results with a child? By criticising them? By yelling at them? By hitting them? Or will a child benefit most by being truly loved? By giving them clear boundaries? By having a conversation or a dialogue with them? It's clear when we see outside of ourselves what creates the best result. But somehow, you think, *If I judge myself harshly then maybe I'll be better, or then maybe I'll do things differently.* Dear soul, it does not work like that. You have to flip it and start with love in order to feel good in your body. If you can't jump straight into love, start with awareness, then move into appreciation, and then into love.

Awareness—Appreciation—Love

If you dig deep enough you can find something to appreciate about your body. Your blood pumps through your body, your heart beats without conscious thought, you can breathe, you can digest food. It's incredible, our bodies are awesome!

Imagine how giving your body appreciation every day would help you feel more comfortable being physically present in your body? If you are feeling good being in your body you will want to stay there, you will want to hang out. Take a deep breath and say: *'I love you, body. You are incredible. Thank you, body.'*

At first it may feel like a lie as you start complimenting your body. It might feel like you're deceiving yourself. Eventually, you can trick yourself into believing good things about yourself that in time become real. This is how manifestation works as well. You start by imagining what you want as if it's real and eventually it becomes real.

When I started to practice body love, in time I lost weight while eating more of the foods that were supposed to be unhealthy, like cake! With self-love, I ate in a kinder way, which for me meant exercising less and eating more 'unhealthy' foods, and the crazy thing is, I lost weight. It didn't make sense. I had been punishing myself with food deprivation and exercise and somehow this was holding the excess weight in place. When I moved my body and ate food from a place of love, the weight melted off my body. This seemed miraculous to me.

Body love starts by simply saying positive things about your body, even if you don't quite believe them. The more you praise your body, the more you will embody what you are saying as the truth.

If you are having a hard time with speaking kind things to your body, imagine saying the negative words you tell yourself to a newborn. Would you even consider doing that? You would never be that cruel to a child. That would be abusive.

It's time to start shifting these patterns within yourself and loving you. When you give yourself a hard time just say, 'Look, I'm doing it again. Oh, I love you, body. Please forgive me.'

High Vibrational Spaces

To help with coming out of hiding and showing up here fully, surround yourself with people and spend time in places where you feel safe to be you. This is your practice ground. These high vibrational spaces give you a place to recharge, reconnect and refuel for when you must go back out into the world again.

Find environments where you feel nurtured. I seek out locations that allow me to rebalance within and with all of life, to recharge my batteries in order go out into the world loves you like a mother, she is your Divine Mother. A mother never wants her child to go without; she wants to support you and help you manifest your desires and experience the fullness that life has to offer. You were created to receive her sustaining life force. This is another powerful practice of receiving.

Take your energy down into the earth. Grow your energetic roots. Roots suck up moisture and nutrients. Your energy can take in Earth energy to nurture your body.

You have to show up to access the full potential of this Earth energy. Mother Earth loves and supports you whether you're present or not but you can draw on her strength in a greater capacity if you are living in your physical expression, which is your body.

We participate in a co-creation with Mother Earth. She's helping you to manifest and to design your life on the physical realm. Ask Mother Earth for what she has to offer you. She is waiting to help you.

When you anchor your light here on the Earth, you share it with the planet. The light you release goes wherever it is needed. As you give to the Earth, you receive from the Earth, and as you receive from the Earth, you give to all creation.

Let's image your WOW goal is a money tree seed. The

seed is filled with what you desire. You need to plant that seed and give the seed the right environment, the soil and the water it requires so it can start sending its roots down and sprouting its little shoots up. The roots strengthen and deepen as the shoot grows up, getting bigger and stronger. Your money tree grows similarly over time. With the right care and attention, eventually you can start feeding from the tree, living on it, being supported from that money tree.

Receiving from the Earth practice

Call on all of yourself present here now in your body, on this planet. Imagine or visualise your energy, your essence, your light filling your body, shooting out through the base of your feet down into the Earth like energetic roots. Imagine taking these roots down, down, down, through the layers of the Earth. If you can, see them going down into the centre of the earth. Envision the energy from Mother Earth, and feel its power. This is an exchange. You gift your energy to the Earth, and she gifts you back with her energy, her love and nurturance. Spend time actualising this energy exchange in your physical being.

This practice will help you to feel more grounded, calm and focused. When you are in this state, you move into a greater place of balance. It feels good and it propels you forward into the process of bringing your manifestations into reality.

End of Chapter Actions

- Practice 'Step 1: Relax', 'Step 2: Release', 'Step 3: Receive' and 'Step 4: Rhythm' Part 1 daily, including receiving from the Earth.
- Call on all of yourself to be here now. Do this every day. Give yourself permission to be aware of, and to welcome, *you*.
- Journal on, *When do you hide yourself? When do you shrink your genuine self?*
- Ask your body, *'Body, how would you like to move today?'* Talk to your body, ask what it wants to do.
- Talk to your body and acknowledge it.

Chapter 6

Step 4: Rhythm Part 2

Guided Action

> *'I never came upon any of my discoveries through the process of rational thinking.'*
>
> – Albert Einstein

Thirteen years ago, I made a promise to myself to always follow my intuition and it has never failed me yet. Following my intuition has led me to create a really magical life. It has brought the life that I could only imagine, but without intuition, I had no idea how to make it happen. Step by step, with courage and patience, I have been intuitively guided towards the life and business of my dreams.

I would like to share with you how you can use your intuition in your personal life and your business and fulfil the longings of your heart and soul.

Taking Action on Inner Guidance

Once you are anchored in your body, the next element of Rhythm is taking *guided action*. This is the practice of listening to your intuition, listening to the guidance from the Universe, your higher self and then taking concrete action in the world based on that guidance.

How many times have you had the urge to do something only to ignore it? Your intuition is speaking to you all of the time but the trick is to actually listen to what it has to say. It's all well and good getting an intuitive message or inner guidance, but it won't change your life for the better unless you take action.

Over the years, I have received many intuitive messages. Some of them I ignored for years. I received the message over and over again to write a book, for example. It has taken me eight years to finally write my first book. This is that book, the one you are reading now. The idea of writing books and being published was something I saw for my future, but I had to follow through on that guidance and do it! Without action you only have imaginings floating around in the ether. If you are a dreamer or visionary like me, that is a fun place to live, but if you don't act on your visions in the physical world, they will stay as they are, unrealised dreams.

Your intuition is what I call the all-seeing, all-knowing part of you. This goes beyond the mind, beyond the personality, beyond your ego. You are tapping into something much, much greater within yourself when connecting to your intuition. Listening to your inner direction is about getting in touch with your higher self, your true essence or your soul.

Following your intuition is about getting into flow with the deeper purpose of your life, the guidance from the Universe and co-creating your destiny here on this planet as a joint venture between your soul and the Universe. Your intuition is here to help you activate your full potential on Earth.

Your mind, your ego and your personality can get in the way of this co-creation and block your inner knowing, block you from being able to feel your innate wisdom. This will stop you from creating the life that deep down you know that you are here to create.

Your mind, ego and personality are a part of this human experience on Earth. Your ego challenges are part of your soul's journey, too. But when you bring your conscious awareness to a recognition of how your ego influences you, the less power it will have. This is where the magic of consciously co-creating your life with the Universe begins.

Following your intuition helps you align with your true path and your true calling. It creates greater success in your personal life and your career, and helps you navigate through the stormy seas. Your intuition is like your own personal lighthouse. Life happens, storms happen, the wind blows, the waves roll, but that inner knowing can help you ride out the challenges that will come. Your intuition helps you to move in harmony with nature rather than fighting against it, and will guide you with clarity and focus rather than just being tossed about with no direction and no mooring.

Your intuition is a part of you. It's the part of you that just knows! The process of learning to listen to your truth and follow it is about trusting yourself, what you know, your gut instinct, even if you can't explain *why*.

You connect to your intuition most effectively by calming the mind, calming the ego and taming your emotions. By doing so you will have the clarity to hear your inner wisdom.

We have already been through the first steps to connecting to your intuition, which are 'Relax', slow down the mind; 'Release', clear the negative thoughts and beliefs; 'Receive', what you are asking for; and 'Rhythm', Part 1, which is to get into the driver's seat of your life. The next step is to discover the various ways your intuition speaks to you.

Your intuition is a part of how you perceive information on the other levels of consciousness beyond the physical realm. You could call this your 'extrasensory perception'. It is a part of your true nature, and I believe everyone can connect to its direction, and yet we haven't been taught to listen to it or trust it. Instead, we have been taught to ignore our intuition and shut it down.

Following your intuition is about allowing yourself to be led and guided by your higher self and the Universe. It's about accepting and creating the life you've always wanted.

Following your intuition is about embodying your inner guidance from the divine, your higher self and the Universe. It's about birthing your dreams, your visions, into reality. You are the one in a physical body so you are the one that needs to take action on that guidance and bring it into the world. Your intuition will 'tell' you how to make more money, but you are the one that will need to act on that 'how'.

Some things you wish to manifest, like money, will just come to you. Money may be gifted to you, for example. By all means welcome that in, say yes to it, but this won't be the only avenue for your dreams to show up into your reality.

I sat around for years waiting for things to come to me. Some did, but some didn't. I was missing the 'taking action' piece on my manifestation journey. I was using the first three steps to 'Abundance Activation': 'Relax', 'Release', 'Receive', but I was missing Step 4. The first three steps alone did work to a degree, but I didn't use Step 4 to get my butt in gear and venture out into the world. Not taking action limited what was possible in my life.

I was getting messages to 'do' things, but those instructions were guiding me to my greatest fears. For example, I got the message for ages that I needed to make videos and post them on social media platforms. I might as well have been asked to jump off a cliff or walk into a fire. I was terrified of this idea. It felt like I was being asked to go to my death. But finally, I faced my fear, felt all the terror and doubt and just did it. I filmed my first videos and posted them, despite my trembling hands. I kept making videos and the more I did this the less uncomfortable I felt. Now making videos is one of my favourite parts of my business.

At this point, I thought the purpose of life was to feel peaceful, calm and centred. So any time I felt fear or doubt, I would assume that I was on the 'wrong' path. It took me a number of years to finally realise that in order to manifest my dreams, I was going to need to get uncomfortable.

The things that will create the greatest result in your life are often found where your greatest fears lie. This is why it's hard to take action on your dreams, as you often have to face your biggest demons. I know, it sucks, but it's part of what makes this journey interesting. The truth is it would be boring if there were no challenge for you. You are here to grow and expand. Stagnation creates misery.

I still use 'Step 1: Relax' every day to return to that place of peace, stillness and balance, but when you are stepping into the unknown, your deepest fears will arise. There is no avoiding deep discomfort when you are starting something new. This is why we keep practicing 'Step 1: Relax' and 'Step 2: Release' every day, to have restoration while facing the fear of the unknown.

You will often not know *why* you are being guided to do something. You may have an idea but you will not necessarily see the full picture. With making videos, for example, I had the feeling that this was about becoming more visible, helping people to find me, and sharing helpful information, but I didn't understand the influence they would have. I still don't! But I have had many messages from strangers sharing the impact that my videos on YouTube and Facebook have had in their life, which makes it all worthwhile.

When you are asking for more money to come into your life, you may be guided to start up a new business, for example, or you may get a new idea. If you already have a business you may get inspiration on how to develop your outreach. Your business can be an avenue for great financial reward. But you will have to take physical action to grow that business. This can take time to develop and will require patience and trust. There are many ways that money can come to you, a career or business are just two examples.

Try not to become overwhelmed by the big vision. All you need to do is take the next baby step. Ask your inner guide: *'What choice can I make today that would produce the greatest result?'*

See what pops into your awareness. Then take action on that message.

Please remember following your intuition is not about getting it right, it's about giving yourself time and space to keep listening, trusting and practicing. You are reprogramming an old way of being, the state in which most people exist. Taking guided action is how you forge a path to all the good that awaits you.

What is your Intuition?

Your intuition is also known as your inner-knowing, your gut instinct, the all-seeing, all-knowing part of you. Your intuition is also guidance from the Universe and your higher self or soul. Your intuition is wisdom from your higher self, your soul and the Universe. Your intuition is a communication from the Universe and your higher self.

Through your intuition you can co-create your life and business with the Universe and your higher self. Following your inner wisdom takes you beyond the mind, beyond the ego, beyond the personality and taps into something much greater within.

Manifestation is made in collaboration with your higher self and the Universe. You are a team player in this process. You will be required to take physical action on this money manifestation journey.

Your intuition will give you the answers to your questions, intentions and prayers. Your intuition guides you towards all that you desire.

The information that comes to you in the present is exactly what you need to hear at this moment on your journey. Your intuition will change as you change, grow, evolve and expand. What comes through to you is what you need to know when you need to know it, as you continue toward your destiny.

Following your intuition is about connecting to the bigger picture of life, taking you beyond the mind, beyond the ego, beyond this 3D reality.

What does your Intuition Do?

Your intuition is with you all of the time. It is your link to your higher self, your soul, and the Universe. You can't cut yourself off from your intuition, it's there with you whether you choose to listen to it or not. You can block out your intuition and numb yourself from being able to feel or hear it, but you can't ever disconnect completely.

Following your intuition helps you to live with greater success. From my experience, both in my own life and by coaching many clients, ego-based decisions don't tend to bring good results.

When you make decisions from your ego, you bring about more pain and suffering. Ego-based decisions can also come with big highs followed by big lows. Your ego will give an experience of separation, competition, lack, scarcity and can leave you feeling unhappy and alone.

Your intuition always comes for your highest good. This means that you will always be guided to the best for your life, your soul's journey, for your purpose here on this Earth.

Your intuition will always guide you to greatness. Your intuition takes you to the best possibility for your life. This greatness, the full potential for your life is beyond what your mind can understand or perceive.

Your intuition has a 360-degree perspective on all of life. This makes your intuition a great problem-solver and can help navigate you through the more difficult problems that life presents. It's impossible to discern the way out of challenging situations from the level of the mind and the ego. Your intuition will show you the way.

By following your intuition, you don't have to figure it all out in your head. When you are tapping into your intuition, you'll have the ability to understand everything that life throws at you. Your intuition will tell you, show you and guide you.

Your intuition is always with you. If you have not been actively listening to your intuition or acknowledging it, it may be hard to 'hear'. Strengthen your relationship with your intuition in order to hear it better. Let's explore the ways your intuition can speak to you.

Jenny's Story

Intuition

I'm a really empathic person who has worked with healing modalities for many years. My intuition guided me to put our house on the market; a much loved home for 20 years, as we were guided to be in a new location.

I made a vision board with photos of our place, a cheque with the amount we intended to attract with an 'or something better' clause! Photos of us looking happy and the words: 'Joy' 'Abundance' 'Freedom' 'Adventure'. Each day feeling deeply the excitement of each sentiment expressed.

It was a huge step to give up a house and life, which had been familiar to us for a long time. Every day I'd walk in the nearby forest, feeling each footstep, breathing deep to assuage any wobbles and relax. My inner child would come out to play. I'd skip and twirl and return to a lightness in my heart. Connection. Love. Freedom. Joy. Abundance.

I did this before our first viewing. My intuition whispered the words: 'Divine Love Prospers Me Now' then I heard the song: 'My love is like a red, red rose'. So I started singing the lyrics to the tune received! This became my daily practice!

The day after going on the market we had a viewing and we received an offer- way below the asking price. I was guided to 'take time for the love to flow and grow'.

We had 19 viewings in 2 weeks. We received 5 offers in total. On the days with more than one viewing, we cleared the energy and I continued with my rhythm of grounding, being present and singing to the Universe, feeling the

Divine Flow deep within my heart. Feeling grateful and connected.

Our house sold for £60,000 over the valuation price. When we received the call to say the sale was finalised from the solicitor we were in a supermarket car park - a 444 JEN registration drove past (means many angels are with you). We walked across to the estate agent and a car with an 888 DAY (means abundance is with you).

Magic and Miracles really do happen when you relax, release, receive, get into the rhythm and repeat it.

Bless you and thank you, Lara, for switching-on my inner Abundance Activation switch.

Jenny Anne Slater
Conscious Moonpause Mentor
http://laforetdesetoiles.com

Psychic Senses, Intuitive Senses

Everyone is able to develop their psychic abilities. It's not a gift that only special people have. We can all tap into higher levels of consciousness that are beyond this 3D reality. It's just a matter of tuning in to a more subtle energetic dimension.

There are a number of ways that your intuition can

come through to you. Often it will speak to you through a combination of these psychic abilities but one of these senses may be stronger than the others.

The 4 Main Psychic Senses

- **Clairsentience—Inner Feeling:** This is connected to the heart-centre. This is when you 'feel' the truth. You feel life through your body. This could also be called your gut instinct.
- **Clairaudience—Inner Hearing:** This is connected to the throat chakra. This is when you hear wisdom. This is similar to hearing voices or hearing words, but this is through your inner sensing, which is different from how your ears hear sound from the outside world.
- **Clairvoyance—Inner Seeing:** Clairvoyance is connected to the brow chakra and is also known as the third eye. This is when you see what is going on in the other levels of consciousness in your mind's eye. Here you are shown images via your inner sight. You may get still or moving images via your inner vision.
- **Claircognizance—Inner Knowing:** This is when you just know something but you can't explain how. Awareness seemingly pops into your head. This is connected to the crown chakra.

These are the four main psychic vehicles by which your intuition can speak to you. Some senses may be stronger than others. If you have been ignoring your psychic impressions, you may feel like you don't possess any of these abilities but it's just a matter of learning to trust and reconnect. Everyone can do this.

Here are the ways that your intuition will speak to you:

Calm—Clear—Neutral

Your intuition will always be calm. Your intuition is never fear based. Your intuition will always be clear—there is no drama. Your intuition will always come to you in an emotionally neutral way.

Lyrics of songs

If you ever have lyrics to a song going around and around in your head, take note of the lyrics. There will be a message for you.

Triple Numbers, Feathers, Lessons in the World Around You.

Intuitive lessons from the world around you can come to you as triple numbers or white feathers. You can receive directions from the world around you, from nature, from animals. Life is communicating to you at all times.

If you receive information that is fear-based or negative, this is not your intuition speaking. Negative information is usually your ego or negative energetic interference. Your inner wisdom will bring you awareness, but it will be energetically neutral.

If you get the same message from a few different unrelated sources, this is the Universe speaking to you, so pay attention.

All of us are unique. Every person will have a special method by which their intuition communicates with them. If you don't know how your intuition speaks to you, not to worry, continue practicing and learning to trust yourself.

How to Follow your Intuition

The first four steps to abundance activation are designed to help you tap into your intuition. While you are learning to trust your intuition, I recommend using the first four steps of 'Abundance Activation' to bring your mind into a clear, balanced, peaceful place so as not to interfere with the incoming guidance from your higher self and the Universe.

'Step 1: Relax' is always the first step. Sit and stop until your mind is calm. If you have emotional triggers or challenges, sometimes it can take longer to relax. Give yourself the time and space you need to get clear and centred.

'Step 2: Release'. If you find blocks you've put up to this process, release these judgements, emotions, thoughts and beliefs. By doing so you are releasing the ego mind. The information from your intuition will often speak to you through your mind, so you want to keep your thoughts and emotions clear and balanced. Remember that your ego self will try to keep you safe from that which it doesn't know. Keep releasing when this happens.

'Step 3: Receive'. Your intuition is always with you and you can tune into it in an instant. Be receptive to the incredible wealth of information and guidance that is ready and waiting for you. All of the answers to your questions, your challenges and your dreams are available to you.

'Step 4: Rhythm' is a daily practice of getting into your body so that you can act on the guidance you receive from your intuition. This is also important if you are clairsentient, receiving intuitive information through feelings in your body. You need to be present in your physical form so that you can feel this instruction. Be aware of your body to create a strong anchor within yourself. This will help to soften the energetic noise around you and help you to get clarity. Many distractions can influence you and draw you out of this process. Come back home to you so you can more accurately determine what is right for you.

Intuition Tips

Let Go: You cannot force your intuition to be active; you have to let go in order to receive it. Don't try, let it happen. Your intuition is there waiting for you to get out of your own way so you can hear it.

Pay Attention: Your intuition will speak to you in many ways. Stay present to how your inner knowing comes. Remember, it can be through words, feelings, visuals or simply an awareness of the answer.

Ask questions: The answers will come based on the questions you ask. Keep your questions as open as possible.

Trust: You may feel like you are making up the answers at first. Your intuition can sometimes feel like it's just a thought in your head. Trust what you get.

Be patient: The 'answers' may not come immediately. Be patient, keep asking and the answers will show up eventually. They do not always show up in the way that you might think so stay open and look for the messages all around you.

Practice: The more you practice listening to your

intuition, the more confident you will be. You are retraining your intuition muscle; the more you exercise it, the stronger it will become.

Follow the Joy: Keep it light, fun and playful. If you get too serious about hearing your intuition this can create a block for you. Play with your intuition as if you can't get it wrong and as if the result doesn't matter. This will help you enjoy the process.

Asking Your Intuition Questions
Yes or No answers. What is a yes? What is a no?

The first step to receiving intuitive information is to ask questions that have a 'yes' or 'no' answer.

Clearing the Way

Before you begin asking your intuition questions, clear your thoughts, emotions and energy, as this will help to produce a distinct answer.

Close your eyes, let go and release.

You can say the following:

'Anything that might be stopping me or blocking me from receiving clear intuitive guidance, I let it go now.'

'Anywhere that I am sabotaging myself from receiving

clear intuitive awareness, I invite all of that to break loose and melt out of my body, into the Earth beneath me, out into the Universe around me.'

You are now going to ask your body, the Universe, your higher self to make it apparent how your intuition communicates with you.

Close your eyes and ask your body...

'*Body, higher self, please show me what is a Yes?'* Breathe and see what you feel. How does that feel in your body? What comes up for you?

Now ask, '*Body, what is a No for me?*' Then see what you feel. How does a No feel in your body?

Then ask again, "*What is a Yes for me and what is a No... make it easy to understand.*" You can play back and forth between a 'Yes' answer and a 'No' answer so you get confirmation on the difference of how that feels in your body.

Light and Heavy

Generally speaking, there's a lightness with a 'Yes' and a heaviness with a 'No'. If it's light, it's right; if it's heavy, then do some investigation around the heaviness. Heaviness doesn't always mean that it's a 'No' answer. Sometimes you need to explore the heaviness. The general rule is, if it's light, it's right.

Everyone will have different sensations in their body when asking what a 'Yes' and a 'No' is. Listen to your body, it will tell you.

Pendulum: A pendulum is a helpful tool when you are having trouble trusting your intuition. It is usually a thin chain approximately 10–12 inches long with a crystal or stone attached at the end. You begin by holding the top of the chain with the crystal dangling below. Ask, *'What is a Yes, show me what a Yes answer is.'* The pendulum will turn either clockwise or counterclockwise. You can then say, *'Show me what is a No'* and the pendulum will turn the other way. Tell the pendulum to show you a 'maybe' or 'ask again'. It will swing in a different way. It's quite magical! A pendulum is a positive way of affirming all that you are learning.

As you play with your intuition, you will be discovering the unique ways that wisdom comes to you. You can receive intuition through feeling, thoughts, visuals, sound or inner knowing. You can also experience a combination of more than one. Your ability to receive will get stronger as you experiment and practice.

Beyond 'Yes' and 'No' Answers

Some questions you will ask your intuition have a clear 'Yes' or 'No' answer, but there are many times your intuition will speak to you without a 'Yes' or a 'No'. It's important to establish a relationship with your intuition for an open communication dialogue so that you can understand whatever information it may have for you.

Your intuition can come to you in a variety of channels. Through a feeling in your body, an inner knowing, visual images in your mind's eye or through words that can seem similar to a dialogue in your head.

The Universe will also bring your answers and information through other people, serendipitous meetings, or opportunities seemingly popping up out of nowhere. Stay receptive to all of the amazing surprises that await you as your intuition gives you direction.

Listening to your intuition is an exploration of the wonderful connection you have. The more attention you give to your intuition, and the more you listen to it, the stronger it will become.

Strengthening Your Intuition

Tune in every day. I recommend having a daily meeting

with your intuition. I call it 'my business meetings with the Universe'. This is a great practice to reset what you think you 'should' be doing and how you 'should' be doing it every day. Your ego self is very strong and will try to take over your life. By checking in daily you are clearing the path, getting out the distractions and making sure that you are going in the direction of the best path forward for you and your life.

If you're still in doubt about the intuitive answers that you are getting, request guidance that is easily interpreted.

Let go of how or when the answer comes. If there is any expectation or tension that appears when tuning into your intuition, release it and await whatever result you are given.

Please note that drugs, alcohol and toxic food will affect your intuition. They are like blockers to your soul. You can help develop your intuition by detoxing your body.

Staying Open—Asking Questions

Your ego mind loves to feel in control, it likes to believe that it understands life and how it works. Your ego draws conclusions and makes judgements about what is and is not possible and how your journey should be, all the time.

Your ego creates walls and closes doors on what is available for you and your life. This is happening whether you like it or not.

Asking questions of your intuition keeps you in a place of receiving. If you have a challenge, there is always a solution; if you have a dream, there is always a way to make it happen, but you may not know what that is yet or how it will appear. Remember, you don't know what you can't access. There are solutions and answers that you have not yet discovered.

When you stay responsive by asking questions, you are in a place of acceptance. You have opened a door on life to let the infinite possibilities in. The ego self does not like this but living in expectation and being receptive is how you make room for your dreams to manifest into your reality.

Stay in the question every day throughout the day. This is when life starts to feel very magical. The gifts are there, ready and waiting for you, and you will be led forward to achieve a life beyond your imagination.

Your Questions Determine the Answer

The questions you ask your intuition will determine what answers you get. When you're sitting and meditating, information may start coming into your head without you even asking questions. But if you ask in specific detail, you will be given a response that is in turn specific to the question.

Your questions are powerful. The answer that comes is based on what you are asking. Please be aware of what you are seeking. You want to be in alignment with your higher self so that you don't create unnecessary pain or misery for yourself and others.

What Choice can I Make that Will Create the Greatest Result?

Ask yourself this question every day: *'What choice can I make that will create the greatest result?'*

What comes to you when you ask that question? Did that question bring an awareness of where you should put your attention? This is good to ask daily to get clarity on where to focus your energy and what action to take that day. You can also ask this question again throughout the day if you need direction.

I love asking this question. Again, your ego will tell you what you should or shouldn't do. When I ask, 'What choice can I make that will create the greatest result?' I am often guided towards the thing that I have the most resistance to doing, as the thing that we have the most resistance to doing will often create the greatest result for my life. Thank you, ego, for trying to keep me safe… now off you go.

When I ask this question, sometimes I get guidance to rest or go for a walk. The answer that comes is not always work-related. Sometimes the best decision you can make is to relax and let go, to play and have fun. Relaxing helps you to connect deeply to yourself, your truth and your purpose.

Keep asking: 'What choice can I make that will create the greatest result?' You may be surprised by what you receive.

What Action can I take Now?

This is a great question to ask to get clarity on the next best action step to take. There will be lots of little baby steps that take you towards realising your goals. What's the next best step you can take now?

So often your ego self tries to take you off track, distracting you from your true path, grabbing your attention with what's bright and sparkly. It's not always the most exciting or creative thing that will create the greatest result for your life. Most successful business people have success and wealth from regular consistent action that you might consider boring. Regular consistent action takes you into the manifestation of your dreams.

What will my Life be like in Five Years if I Choose this?

If you have a major decision to make, or any decision for that matter, this is a great tool to shed light on the results of that decision. I learned the power of this question a number of years ago, and I use it often.

When tuning into your intuition, there may not be a clear yes or no answer to your questions but there will be a choice that will create a greater future reality for you. To help get clarity on which choice will create the greatest result, ask:

'What will my life be like in five years if I choose this? What *will my life be like in five years if I don't choose this?'*

This question is designed to tap into the possibilities ahead of the decision you are considering. When you ask this, close your eyes and see what awareness comes to you.

What Blocks Your Intuition?

It takes trust to listen to your intuition and follow it. Many obstacles can come up to block you from hearing your intuition. Be aware of how you may prevent this process. When these hindrances show up, go back to 'Step 2: Release' to sweep them away.

Here are some of the intuition pitfalls…

Listening to other people's opinions and judgements: You may have an idea to do something that feels right for you. If you share this idea with someone, they might tell you all the reasons why it won't work. They can end up projecting their judgements, fears, experiences and points of views onto you, which can cause you to doubt yourself. Use discernment when considering whom to share your intuitive wisdom with. It's easy to be influenced by your environment and the people around you.

Expanding your comfort zone: When you start to take steps towards making your dreams a reality, you are expanding your comfort zone beyond what you know or have experienced. Anytime you try to move beyond your comfort zone, your friend 'the ego' rises up to stop you. Be aware that your ego self can go bananas when there's a threat to what it considers familiar. Your deepest fears, doubts and insecurities will often flare up in these moments. When this happens go back to 'Step 1: Relax' and 'Step 2: Release' to restore your inner peace. I also recommend reaching out to your support team as they will encourage you to release and keep moving forward.

Trying to get it right: On the higher levels of consciousness there is no right or wrong. Right and wrong, good or bad, in the way that we perceive it in our world, does not exist beyond this physical dimension. This is a difficult concept for the mind to grasp because our ego likes life to be black and white and to put everything into neat and tidy little boxes, but life doesn't work like that. You can end up being paralysed and unable to change if you are looking for the 'right' way to do life. Your soul's journey, why you are here and what you are being asked to do, functions from a different dimension of consciousness.

Your soul is leading you to greatness, to the full expansion and expression of who you are and what you are here to do and experience on this planet. When you are listening to and following your intuition, you will always be brought into greatness.

Don't worry if you veer too far off course, you will get the message! Your intuition is much like Sat Nav. If you take a 'wrong' turn, you will be redirected. The truth is you can't make a wrong turn, so please don't put pressure on yourself to get it right.

Divine Timing

We have talked about the psychic senses and the various ways that information comes to you but there is also something called divine timing. Divine timing is where things happen at the right time, at the right place, for your soul's journey. You cannot force your dreams to materialise faster than you would like. This will only create frustration, pain and suffering. The hard truth is some things that you are asking for may take longer than you would like to show up, and some things that you are asking for will show up completely different from what you imagined. This is why it is so important to trust and let go.

Divine Meetings

You will also experience divine meetings, opportunities that seemingly spring up out of the blue. This is another way that the divine can manifest into your life.

Divine Gifts

Gifts may come into your life. You may be unexpectedly given things. Welcome them!

Ideas will come to you (write them down!)

Ideas might enter into your head out of nowhere. Be sure to write them down because they may be pertinent now, or later. Record them so you don't forget. I always carry a little notebook with me to jot down my ideas. They can come at the funniest, most inopportune times, like when I am on the toilet! Be ready to catch those unexpected inspirations.

You don't need to know HOW

You don't need to know how things are going to happen. This can be hard for your ego mind to accept. When you receive direction from your intuition, you don't need to know how you are going to make it happen, you just need to hold the intention. The same with your money goals, you do not need to know how it's going to happen, you just need to listen because you'll be given little bread crumbs from the Universe to follow… and eventually as you move on, baby step by baby step, your path will become clearer. Lots of little steps will take you to where you want to go, eventually.

You don't need to know WHY

You may not know 'WHY' you are being guided towards something or why you are being guided away from something. You don't need to know why; in fact, in many situations it will be impossible to know why. In time, all will become clear. This is the practice of trust.

You may not always get a clear black and white answer from your intuition. Different choices yield different results. Your intuition is keeping you in alignment with the bigger picture of your life and your soul's purpose.

I am often guided in my business with directions and I don't know why. Sometimes I have a sense of why I am given these instructions, but I can't see the full picture. Over time I have learned to become comfortable in this uncertain place. Through experience I have learned that I am always being guided towards the next best thing. I am always being led to grow and expand to the next level. It is not always easy moving into the unknown, but it always results in greatness and I have come to rest in that truth.

Big Decisions

Keep checking in with big decisions that you are considering. When there are decisions to be made that mean greater change in your life, the ego can start interfering. You want to be sure that you have cleared your fears, doubts, judgements and opinions before making a commitment. I recommend double-checking a number of times to make sure you have clarity on the situation. The ego is sneaky and likes to find a way to sabotage positive change. The ego can sometimes seem like intuition. You want to be certain that the decision you are going to make is in alignment with your purpose.

Intuition Can Be Like the Weather

Sometimes the intuitive guidance that you receive in one moment will take a different direction over time. Sometimes you'll be told something, be guided to do something and then it will change if you tune in again. Life is always in flux. Your intuition can be like the weather. This is part of the ever-changing nature of life.

When listening to your intuition, some messages will be distinct and some messages can be more nebulous, so you want to continue to focus inward until you have certainty. You can say yes to something that feels right in one moment, and then over time you might feel right saying no. This is okay as situations can shift. This is confusing for the personality part of you, but with patience, it will all make sense.

Taking Action Guided By Your Intuition

After you receive guidance, the next step is taking physical action on that intuition. This is the practice of allowing what you are asking for to manifest into reality.

This is acting in alignment with your higher self, your soul and your intuitive guidance. What steps are you being guided to take?

Your dreams need to manifest into this physical reality and this can happen through your physical activity. Your desires may also manifest through other people or other situations, but this support often shows up when you are listening and doing.

Life flows more easily when you are guided by your intuition. When you take action (or no action) based on your ego, life does not go in a forward direction so easily. This is when we experience greater pain, suffering and stress.

What you are Asking for is on the Other Side of your Comfort Zone

I have found that for the most part, the action that you will be guided to take is often outside of what is comfortable. On my personal journey, I have been guided to do many things that have terrified me. Following your dreams can be uncomfortable and scary, but you need to face that discomfort if you are going to have the reality you are here to enjoy.

It's amazing to me how often what you truly want can bring up the most discomfort. This is because in order to create a different future, you need to start making different choices and taking different action in the NOW.

The ego does not like the unknown. The ego perceives anything that it does not understand as a danger and will do everything in its power to stop you. Interestingly, it's the fear of what you are being directed towards that brings the most struggle, rather than the thing itself.

NOTE: Just because something shows up in your reality doesn't mean that you have to say yes to it. TUNE IN first!

The Universe will bring you many opportunities, gifts and

possibilities when you are ready to receive. A variety of possibilities may show up as an answer to what you are asking. I recommend questioning whether this opportunity benefits your goals. It's okay to say no. Just because something has landed in your life doesn't mean you have to go for it. Find a place of stillness, go within and listen for direction.

What You Choose Creates Your Reality

There is no judgement on the higher levels of consciousness, just choice, pure creative energy. Your decisions create your reality; whatever you choose will make a different experience. People often choose to experience a lot of awful things, not consciously, but on some level they are responsible. It's time to get into the driver's seat of your life and start making choices in alignment with what your heart and soul truly want.

You can always make a different choice. Your intuition is like Sat Nav; if you go off course, you will be directed back.

What's cool is that you can make a choice and you can experience the result of that choice and then you can reflect on that choice. Did you like that experience? Yes or No? If you didn't like the result, you can always make a different choice. This is the joy of being in the body and being in life, the pleasure of playing with different experiences. You can choose something, experience that thing, and decide whether you want to keep choosing that as your reality.

If you go too far off, you will know because it won't feel good. Life won't flow. Everything in life has a right time and place. What's joyful and right for you at one point might not be joyful or right for you at another. You are evolving. So just know that you can choose something and then you can choose again if you want another experience.

What's the next little baby step you are being asked to take? Follow the breadcrumbs. These little steps are leading you towards what you want. Sometimes you will make big leaps, when you will be asked to jump high, far and long. These are pivotal moments in your life. But for the most part there are lots of baby steps that will be taking you to where you want to go. This is where you might want to call on patience.

There is always the possibility of your dreams manifesting in an instant; stay open to that of course, but most of life will be made up of incremental moves forward. If you keep taking consistent action, eventually you will achieve the reality you've always imagined.

Listening to your intuition is a practice. Following your inner wisdom is play, because anytime you take it seriously, it won't come so freely. For me, following one's intuition is a joyful, fun, light way of being in the world.

Being guided by your intuition is a learned ability, so be patient with yourself. Most people are making choices based on what's in their head, their emotions, ego, or what they think they should be doing due to family and societal pressures. It may take time to get in the habit of creating your life from this new way of being.

Following your intuition is about tapping into *your* truth and what is true for *you* and *your* path.

Choosing Ease and Joy

I like to include 'with ease and joy' in everything I want to manifest so there isn't unnecessary pain, suffering or struggle. For example: 'What would it take to manifest _____ with ease and joy?'

This question helps you stay out of unconscious drama and sorrow.

Remember that you don't need to know the how. You just need to ask questions to receive the right guidance and navigate your way through life with greater ease and joy.

Healing through Action

On your journey, you will sometimes bump up against your greatest fears, doubts and pain. I have found that the greatest transformation of your money blocks can come through action. Taking action is the most powerful way to free yourself of your fears. Sometimes it's the only way through!

Please don't wait to feel calm, relaxed and comfortable before you act. The sooner you face your fears, the sooner they will loosen their grip on you. Your strongholds will get easier to manage with practice. I promise! Feel the fear and do it anyway.

Life Won't Always Bring You Roses

We have been speaking about creating a life of abundance and joy, and I am sorry to be the bearer of bad news, but darling one, life is not always going to be easy. This journey of leading an intuitively led life can be challenging.

We have been focused on ease, joy, flow and abundance because most people create unnecessary pain and struggle for themselves, but following your intuition does not mean that life won't be hard sometimes.

You will be thrown curve balls, you will get shocks, you will experience loss, hurt and uncertainty. This is life, dear one. This is part of our human experience on this planet. There is no way around this. But, you can reduce the negative impact of these experiences by using the '5 Steps' in this book. 'Step 1: Relax' and 'Step 2: Release' alone will transform any negative experience in your life into one of much greater ease. I didn't say it would be easy, though.

Sometimes the challenges life brings to you are exactly what you need to face in order to move towards your dreams. Life will put your blocks before you so you can be fully aware of them in order to let them go. This is not fun, but necessary.

There will be stormy seas, there will be rough weather, but whatever is showing up for you, just remember, this too will pass.

Finding Support

Finding support on this 'Abundance Activation' journey is essential. It took me a long time to learn this. Get yourself some hand-holding through the changes you make. What you are asked to do from your intuitive guidance is not always comfortable or easy. What you will be asked to do is not always difficult, it's just that deep emotional and mental patterns, once triggered, can stop you from moving forward. Compassion and encouragement will help you through these challenging times in order to take those next steps.

Your fears can stop you dead in your tracks and sabotage your dreams. Because of this it's essential to get support when in transition. Receiving positive assistance will allow the journey towards your dreams to go much faster and be much smoother. We all need something to lean into. Getting help is not a weakness, it's a strength, and one that will be invaluable to you on your money manifestation journey.

I am all about finding support in everything I do. I hire coaches and mentors for anything that I need help developing. The transformation in my life has been amazing as a result.

The things that I really need help with are the things that I haven't done before or things that are not strengths. I find that when I am guided to do what I don't know how to do, or what I haven't done before, my little ego self can become terrified and stop me. It's not that I can't do what I need to on my own, it's just that often I won't. I can unconsciously sabotage myself from moving forward into the unknown. Getting outside help makes the path easier.

Encouragement is important because stepping out of your comfort zone and moving beyond where you are now to where you want to be can be frightening. There is often a strong pull to stop the momentum. Sometimes you just need someone to take your hand and tell you that you can do it. It's like having a midwife when you are giving birth. The midwife isn't going to give birth to the baby, you are, but she is there stroking your back reassuring you that you can do it.

Who or What can Help Me with this?

This is one of my favourite questions. When you have a new idea, project or challenge, ask your intuition: *'Who or what can help me with this?'*

Sometimes the answer will pop into your mind right away and sometimes it will take time for the answer to show up. Emotional support can show up in many ways. You are always infinitely supported by the Universe. There is also practical physical support that comes from other humans or from technology. Recognise where your strengths are and when you need to reach out. You were never meant to travel this journey alone.

The Greatest Version of You and Your Life

Through your connection to the Universe and your higher self, you are always being guided to greatness. Your intuition will always lead you to the best version of you and your life.

Your intuition leads you beyond the mind, beyond your emotions, beyond your ego, beyond all the family and societal programming of how you should live your life. Your intuition directs you on your soul's journey.

Soul's Desires vs. Your Desires

There is a dance between what you are asking for on the personality level and what your soul is here to experience. There is space for both aspects of you to be realised. Your life will benefit when the majority of your choices are in alignment with your higher self, your soul's path. Generally, if something brings you joy and makes you feel lighter, it's in alignment. If something makes you really unhappy, usually it's not in alignment. It's important to do the inner connecting work to get clear on what you are being asked to do and what you are being asked to surrender. The more you can commit to this current of purpose, the greater your life will become.

Your Soul Does Not Require Money

The soul does not need money. Money is an aid for your physical body. It's okay to include your physical needs in your soul's journey as you are in a physical body! Money is a part of our current reality on this planet. You are allowed to play with having money. This journey is like a game, an exploration. The magic of life is in the adventure.

Welcome In the New

Let go of the old to bring in the new. What you are asking for is a new version of your reality as you have known it. You can't drag the past with you into this dimension. On an energetic level, you are asking to experience a level of consciousness that you have not yet known. Cast off the old way of living that is no longer serving you. If you want a new relationship with money, welcome in financial abundance by turning away from lack and fear of not enough.

Bringing in your new financial reality is about letting go of the old way of labouring in order to welcome in the new way of simple acceptance. Birth isn't always comfortable but it doesn't have to be painful. The more you can let go and get into flow, the easier the transition is, the easier that birth can be.

Failure

You need to be willing to fail in life if you are going to succeed. Think of a toddler learning to walk. How many times does a child need to fall in order to be able to walk? Do we consider the toddler a failure? Of course not. As humans, we learn from failure, we learn from getting things 'wrong'. This is how we grow.

In truth, there isn't failure, there is just feedback. I know how frustrating it can be when things don't work out as you want, but if you can take every situation, every result as feedback, how can you use this as a learning experience?

Take any unnecessary pressure off yourself to 'get it right' and transition instead into the space of exploration and play. Be willing to learn, to fall down, to discover, to get back on your feet and try again. This brings back the wonder in life and will help you to develop in ways you never imagined possible.

End of Chapter Actions

- Practice 'Step 1: Relax', 'Step 2: Release', 'Step 3:

Receive', 'Step 4: Rhythm' Part 1 and 2 daily.
- Play with the Yes/No intuition tools. Ask questions around what food to eat, what to drink, which direction to go, what activities to do. Start asking questions about things that aren't such a big deal to begin with.
- Buy a pendulum if you want help with intuition.
- Journal with your intuition. Some people find that they get intuitive answers best through writing. Explore through journaling.
- See what comes when you sit still and ask your intuition questions.
- Keep releasing when your mind/emotions get in the way.
- Keep it light!
- Add to your vision board: *'What choice can I make today that will create the greatest result? Who or what can help me with this?'*

Chapter 7

Step 5: Repeat

Your Daily Practice—Committing To Change

'Repetition is the Mother of learning, The Father of action, which makes it the architect of accomplishment.'

– Zig Ziglar

Now that you have the first four steps, the final step to 'Abundance Activation' is to repeat Steps 1 to 4 each and every day. These tools work, and they work well if you use them on a regular, consistent basis.

I have magically manifested money into my life many, many times. I say magically because it always feels like magic. To be able to create your life from your intention is beyond the usual, dull routine. I know this manifestation stuff works but I still get excited every time when what I am asking for shows up.

If you really want to change your financial reality, make a commitment to these '5 Steps to Abundance Activation' each day. Make a commitment to spend time with money every day. Energy flows where your attention goes.

5 Steps to Abundance Activation—Recap

Let's review the 5 steps to Abundance Activation:

Step 1: Relax—Meditate or lie down for 10 to 20 minutes or until your mind has slowed down.

Note: This can take longer, especially if there is a lot going on in your life.

Step 2: Release—Money Mindset Mop out; let go of everything standing in the way of receiving.

Step 3: Receive—Open up to receive money and all of the good things in life; breathe money in, become money, fill your golden wealth pot.

Step 4: Rhythm—Be present in your body, move your body, take guided action.

Step 5: Repeat—Do the first 4 steps daily.

In total allow 20 to 30 minutes for this practice each day. Put this in your diary now!

Caroline's Story

'Step 5: Repeat' seems so simple, until the moment you realise you have stepped out of a good routine and habit, while being away on vacation or otherwise busy.

It does take practice, and sometimes other things come up. Recently, I restarted my daily routine of Lara's 5

Steps, and wow amazing, I feel more powerful and more in the flow again. I did not realise that I slipped away little by little, till I was back in it, and felt the difference it all makes.

Caroline Palmy
Angel Healing and Readings
https://palmyhealing.com

Money Journal—How Much Money are you Manifesting?

In your money journal, I would like you to list all the money that comes in, even if it's finding a penny on the floor. Money manifestation shows up in all sorts of interesting ways! You may not notice how money shows up for you, which is why it's helpful to write it down. Include your income and any other funds that come into your life. This can also be in the form of gifts, like someone offering to pay for your lunch, for example. Money manifestation doesn't always appear in the form of money itself, what you are asking for can come in lots of different ways. Stay alert and write it down.

Money Manifestation Mistakes—Getting Rid Of Money

I have manifested money and other great things into my life many times. In the early days, I was motivated to use my money manifestation tools from a place of fear and desperation. I would get myself into a very tight financial situation, then use my money manifesting tools every day. Over a relatively short amount of time, money would come in and then I would relax. When I relaxed, I stopped using my money manifesting tools, and guess what? The money dried up. It has taken the cycle of feast and famine a number of times for me to finally learn from this.

You need to keep feeding the money manifestation fire. A fire requires you to keep putting logs on to keep burning. Money requires you to keep giving it your focus, attention and love to keep growing. Please don't do what I did and stop the practices when money starts coming in. Keep growing your money mountain.

Why did I stop manifesting money once I had it? Well, I realised that there was only so much that I was comfortable receiving. It felt intense to receive and have money. I found it uncomfortable. Crazy, I know! Because of my discomfort with having money, as soon as money came in, I would celebrate by getting rid of it. Then the whole cycle would start up again. I used the lack of money to motivate myself to manifest more. It was a game of lack and create, lack and create, but I got bored of this game. I learned that money can leave as quickly as it comes if you don't take care of it.

Learning to love and care for money, to have and hold money was about learning to love and value myself. Allowing myself to have abundance was a lesson in how to be with myself, my power, my essence and my truth. Having money is about connecting to the most sacred, powerful, sensual part of who I am and letting myself simply be. No more shrinking away or hiding.

'Abundance Activation' and 'Money Manifestation' is a journey of growth and expansion. As you move forward on this journey, you deepen your connection with yourself, the Earth, the Universe and humanity. 'Money Manifestation' in alignment with your soul's purpose is a rewarding, powerful journey. It's not always easy, but it is so worth it.

Money Mindfulness—Monthly Money Dates

We spoke about bringing your attention to money. Money needs your focus, your attention, your energy. The first step (probably the most practical! I get this from my accountant dad) is to know exactly how much money is coming into your life and how much money is going out.

This is a practice of bringing your full attention and consciousness to your financial life. How can you change your financial reality if you are not aware of what is presently in your accounts?

Get yourself a spreadsheet. Keep it simple. On this spreadsheet I want you to list all of the money coming in to your life and all of the money going out, every week or month. Put a date in your diary when you are going to do this. You may need a few hours to complete each session.

Gather all of your bank statements, credit card bills, any other debt you have and make a list of everything you spend your money on down to the penny. Make a note of the cash you spend as well. All card transactions will be on your bank statement. Have a separate column for each category such as food, water, rent, gas, electricity, clothes, going out, eating out, debts, etc. Then do the same for your income.

Now add it all up to find out if you are spending more than you are bringing in, or if you have money remaining at the end of each month.

When I did this I was surprised to see that I was overspending each month. I was totally unconscious when it came to spending. I had a rough idea of how much money was coming in and going out of my life but I didn't want to engage in the reality. Once you know the state of your finances on a practical level, you will know what has to change in the short term to shift your money flows. From this place, you will know exactly what you need and what to ask for. If you are overspending now, make choices to cut back on your spending to correct that shortfall. Keep using your money manifestation tools to ask for more while you honour what is happening in the now.

As a part of my money manifestation magic, I was led to a woman named Ann Wilson, *The Wealth Chef*. Ann taught me all of the practical, grounded information about money I needed. I highly recommend her book, *The Wealth Chef*, to help you with the practical methods of handling money and creating financial freedom.

Chapter 8

Money Manifestation Mastery Reminders

'When you let go, the magic begins.'

– Lara Waldman

Let Go of Control

Did I mention that I am a recovering control freak? Letting go has not been easy for me. My default state was not to trust in others and that made it difficult to trust that I was taken care of. My personal practice has been to keep coming back to surrender and trust. It's something that I have to remind myself to do most days.

Letting go of control is an essential part of money manifestation. The Universe wishes to gift you everything that you desire, but you must get out of your own way to let in what you are asking for. Control patterns are like energetic walls. They give you the illusion of protection and safety but they actually block what you are seeking.

Letting go is the practice of getting out of your own way. You are letting go of what you think you know, what you think life is, what you think it all means, in order to let in the new and the magical, in order to welcome in what is truly possible for you beyond the reach of your conscious mind.

Letting go is also about releasing the thoughts, beliefs and emotions that are blocking your divine flow of financial abundance. Letting go is not something you do once and then forget. From my experience, it's a daily practice and often a moment-to-moment practice.

What you are asking for exists in a different dimension from where you are now. Your dreams reside in a different reality from where you are now. What you are requesting may not be that different from your current situation or your past experiences, it may be just around the corner. But equally, what you are asking for may be very far removed from what you grew up with or what you have now.

In order to welcome in this new reality, you have to step out of your present reality. It's a death of the old way of being in order to birth in the new. If you are clinging to your old patterns, it's like keeping one foot on the shore and one foot on a boat ready to take you to a new land. You can't sail out to those distant shores if you don't step aboard.

Would you be willing to let go of control to let in the new? There is a saying, 'Let Go, Let God', meaning trust in the divine, in the Universe, to bring you what you are asking for, then trust in yourself to take the action necessary to make your dreams a reality.

It takes courage to move forward into the unknown. You are entering a new frontier. This can bring up real feelings of fear, doubt and not feeling safe.

Take a deep inhale, let go with the exhale. Everything is going to be okay, I promise you. Keep breathing, keep relaxing and accepting what is possible. All is well.

Trust

You are being asked to operate in blind faith. Even though I have many, many examples of how these 'Abundance Activation' steps work, I still don't know exactly how my dreams are going to manifest. My little voice of doubt still sneaks in to steal my resolve when I enter into new territory. You need trust and determination to keep going, even though you won't always know how your intentions will appear in physical form.

Keep clearing away the doubt and mistrust, knowing that you are taking the next steps into your new financially abundant, worry-free life.

Your soul, your higher self and the Universe has a 360-degree perspective. Your wee ego mind wears blinders and operates from a limited point of view. There is a way to make your dreams come true. If you can dream it, it's possible.

Patience

Money manifestation requires patience. With manifestation, some things show up relatively quickly while others take time. Hold fast to your vision for the long haul, as it may not happen as soon as you might like. It will be worth the wait.

Tara's Story

When I first started using Lara's Money Manifestation tools, all my fears were brought up then blown away like little dark clouds, giving me moments of realisation and sudden beams of understanding. I practiced the techniques and followed the meditations she guided me through, each time revealing another aspect to my blockages, and opening the way for more flow. By the end of the course, my self-worth had increased dramatically. I have more than doubled my coaching fees, redesigned my website and public profile and become absolutely aligned with my greater calling.

Lara's 'Abundance Activation' steps moved heaps and

mounds of obstacles that I believe were preventing me from wealth and deeper inner fulfilment with my work.

Lara's techniques greased the way for my growth and expansion, and I am now about to publish my first book and launch a worldwide campaign as I have always dreamed. I'm now ready, thanks to Lara, to play the bigger game that my soul always longed to play.

Money and manifesting has been portrayed as something complex and difficult to attain until now, only for the elite and few, but Lara opens the door for a new way to relate to these things. I think we are entering an alternative, new generation of what it means to be wealthy and how to get money, and it's by way of the heart, not greed and ego. Lara brings something unique and special to the world.

Tara Love Perry
Spiritual guide, Soul Reader and Author
www.taraloveperry.com

Why Some Dreams Take Time to Manifest

The main reason why things don't show up as soon as you would like is that your money blocks are at work. Even if you are releasing regularly, some of your negative beliefs may still be in effect. This can be frustrating but it's normal. Please have love, patience and compassion for the part of you that is clinging to the old way of being. This part is terrified of change. This is why it's so important to keep doing the 5 steps every day so you can dislodge those blocks faster and not stay trapped in resistance. You might have to change some deeply embedded habits. Be kind and patient with yourself on this journey.

The other reason your dreams can take time to manifest is just that they take a while to manifest physically. When a house is being built, the foundation must first be laid. It may look like very little is happening at this stage. Then up pops the rest of the house relatively quickly. Your new financial freedom may require time as you lay its foundation.

There is also divine timing in your plan. Manifesting your dreams is a part of your soul's journey and it is so much greater than your personality self. This is why you need trust. All is unfolding as it should.

Hold on to your vision and keep taking that next step. As you move towards your dreams, your dreams move towards you.

I promise you that no matter how long it takes, this money manifestation journey is worth it. Never give up. There is always a way through.

'What you seek is seeking you.' – Rumi

Perseverance

You need to be willing to do whatever it takes to have the life you desire. This is not achieved by force, it's by identifying your WHY to overcome every obstacle and challenge. There will be times when you want to give up. There may be times when it all feels too hard. This is where you need to dig deep, get support and persevere.

Show Up in Your Life

The willingness to fully show up in your life is about taking charge. Take control in order to transform your life. This too is a practice, and it requires daily reminding to be here in your life, in your body. Please be kind and gentle with yourself as you go along your journey.

Support

You were never meant to do this alone. Please find help on your money manifestation journey. Team up with a friend, hold each other accountable. Share your wins, share your fears, your frustrations and your money blocks. Choose someone who is asking for more in their life and willing to step up and take action. Getting support is about receiving what you need to succeed. Together we are more powerful than alone.

Money and Power

Take a moment to step into that WOW amount of money that would blow your mind. Become that abundant for a moment. Imagine yourself with that money. Feel into your body. How does it feel to embody that?

I experience great wealth as power, a deep powerful force within. Most people I speak to fear their power. There is that great Marianne Williamson quote: *'Our deepest fear is not that we are inadequate. Our deepest fear is that we are powerful beyond measure.'*

You have seen examples of the misuse of power, and have chosen not to be that. People have done awful things throughout history. So we fear becoming this.

When I first started to embody my power, I feared I would hurt others with it, that I would act out. What I realised was that this ability is like having a loaded gun. You can harm others with it, but it's about trusting yourself to know when and how to use the gun. Just because you have a weapon does not mean you are going to go on a killing spree. It only means you have protection if it's needed.

Power is like fire; fire is not good or bad, it is simply a force of nature. Fire can burn, destroy and kill or fire can heat your home, cook your food and comfort you as you sit gazing into it. Fire can be used to create pain or pleasure. It all depends on how you use it.

Connecting to your power is about learning how to use it. Power is a transformational energy. How would you like to use the strength and ability that are within your reach? What could you create with this energy?

If you are unsure of what your power is or how to connect to it, after 'Step 1: Relax', when your mind and body are in greater balance, ask: *'Show me my power. What is the purpose of my power?'*

See what comes into your intuitive awareness.

I know that the people I am here to serve are heart-centred and want to make a positive difference on this planet. I trust that you will use your power to create positive change in your life and the lives of others. Fear not, powerful being. You have this strength for a reason. Use the force.

Divine Feminine Power

The deeper purpose of this work is to address a major imbalance that has been continuing on our planet for too long now. There is an ancient energy that has been squashed, suppressed, used and abused. The time has come to bring this wisdom out of hiding and into the light. This is the energy of the divine feminine.

Within us we have both the divine feminine energy and the divine masculine energy. The masculine and feminine energies are different but equally powerful. You can also call these energies the Yin and Yang. We need both balanced within us for greater peace and harmony.

Mother Nature is the embodiment of the divine feminine. The divine feminine energy can destroy. She can take you down in an instant via volcanoes, tsunamis, floods, forest fires, earthquakes, tornados. She is wild and ruthless. But equally Mother Earth feeds us, bathes us, warms us with the sun, and brings us much beauty in nature. She cares for us. She holds us. We couldn't be enjoying this physical experience if it wasn't for Mother Earth. She is our mother, she is home.

However you may judge the powerful aspect of the feminine energy, it is necessary to sustain life. The time is now to reignite this energy. We have fallen out of balance with the masculine and feminine energies and must reclaim that harmony if we want to remain on this planet.

How do you control a population? One way is to take down the feminine; you disempower her and shut her down. How do you do that? You shut off her sexual energy. You make her natural sexual energy wrong, bad, sinful. You set up society so that women are disempowered sexually and financially. You teach her that she is weak and ineffective.

Women have learned to hide their energy. As each woman reclaims herself, her truth, her power, we send ripples of transformation around the globe.

The Dalai Lama said, *'The world will be saved by the western woman.'* How do you think us western women are going to do that? By staying small and broke? Stuck in survival mode? No, my beautiful friend, by empowering yourself, by stepping up, by enjoying life, by freeing yourself financially so you can get on with your purpose and the joy of living.

The divine feminine energy creates differently from the divine masculine. The masculine is all about action, drive, focus, it seeks, it hunts, it penetrates, it's the force of the arrow. We need that energy to get things done and make things happen. But our society has gone too far into adapting the masculine way of being. The divine feminine is the polar opposite, the feminine is open, expansive, intuitive, embracing, holding, welcoming, she draws life towards her.

When we are focusing on money manifestation we need the masculine when taking action, but the remaining money manifestation practices are done through the energy of the divine feminine.

The divine feminine energy is about drawing money towards you, in a seemingly effortless way. The feminine pulls in, draws towards her, seducing life in, while simply being. How nice does that sound, being able to make money by relaxing and seemingly doing nothing!

Women have been trying to conduct life and business the way men operate. This doesn't work best for the female body. The women who use these means are stressed, tight, angry, shut down, tense, and hard. It doesn't feel good. I know this because I operated in this masculine way for a long time, which created imbalance and illness in my body and emotions.

Women create best when they include a place of play, softness, lightness, space, rest, relaxation, connection and peace. Because our society has forgotten how to create in this way, you will need to remind yourself regularly that you are designed to function in the feminine.

Since I was stronger in the masculine for most of my

life, I have to remember to return to this softer feminine energy. Everything flows to me more easily when I work from a balanced masculine and feminine energy. When I become hard and start forcing life, things don't flow as well for me and it definitely doesn't feel good.

When I am tense, anxious, stressed or overwhelmed, I have moved out of the current. I then move back into 'Step 1: Relax'. I sit in meditation or lie down until the chaos and tension melt out of my mind and body. I then move to 'Step 2', which is releasing any thoughts, emotions or beliefs contributing to these negative states, then in 'Step 3', I receive. Ah. My body relaxes and I realise everything I am asking for is already there, waiting for me. The answers are there. I then move to 'Step 4: Rhythm', which is coming home to myself, to my body, and taking gentle, sensual guided action to birth this vision into reality. This is a very joyful way to make money.

Own the Throne

It's time for you to step into who you truly are. It's time for you to step into your body and own your power. How does a wealthy person carry themselves? How does a Queen carry herself? Does she shrink, cower, hide? Hell no! That wealthy Queen owns her throne. She stands strong in who she is. Proud, confident, self-assured. She knows who she is. She knows her value and her worth.

I want you to practice owning your throne. Fake it until you make it.

I used to be an actress. In any new acting job you first read the script. Then we would get together as a cast and do a script reading. After that reading, we would act out the script, we would block out where we were on stage. Eventually, we would know the dialogue by heart, and eventually, would embody our character. Opening night, we were no longer pretending, and I was that character on stage.

As you begin practicing these principles, it may be like those early stages of rehearsing a play, a bit fumbly, not quite right, but eventually, with enough practice, you will become what you envision, you will own that throne and fully embody all that you are meant to be.

Practice stepping into your Queen energy every day, and your King energy if you are a man. It feels great and it's lots of fun.

Money and Pleasure

How much pleasure will you allow yourself? Money and pleasure are deeply linked. Money and sexuality are also linked. Energetically, I experience money coming through the body and out through the genitals. The energy of finances flows through your genitalia, then down your legs and out through your feet. This pleasurable energy of wealth runs through your body, out into the Earth to all life around you.

Will you allow yourself to be turned on? To come alive? To be sensual? Magnetic? Attractive? Desired?

We are taught that money is dirty. We are taught that sex is dirty. We are taught as women that our sexuality is shameful. To love sex is wrong, that makes you a slut. To love money is wrong, that makes you sinful and greedy. To be a highly sexual, rich woman is most definitely wrong!

Perhaps you shut off your sexual energy because you didn't feel safe. Maybe you drew in too much unwanted attention from men and jealousy from women. One of the ways to deal with this is to close off your sexual energy. Spend time examining your relationship to sex and see how this may connect to your relationship with money.

Sexuality is your power, sexuality is your pleasure, your sexuality is an expression of who you are. Your sexuality is creativity, your life force energy, the expression of you. Welcoming wealth into your life is connected to embracing your sexuality and welcoming in pleasure.

If you have been cut off from your true sexual essence, part of healing your relationship with money can include reconnecting to your true sexual nature. This is beyond the physical act of sex. Sex is one form of expressing your sexuality, but your sexual essence can be present regardless of whether you are having sex or not. Your sexuality is your essence, your unique energy, your power, your gift.

Many people have shut off from their true sexuality, or have their sexual wires crossed. Part of welcoming in more money is about embracing your sexuality. As you move through life, breathe your awareness into your sexual being. Bring your focus there.

Part of welcoming more financial abundance into your life with ease and joy is about welcoming greater pleasure into your life. How can you welcome more pleasure into your life?

True Wealth

I would love for you to become as wildly wealthy as you wish. Whatever brings you joy. But *true wealth* lies within. My hope for you is that you discover the great riches that are within you right now. The abundance that is *you*. The connection to your true wealth within will bring you the fulfillment you are searching for. From this place, everything you create and call into your physical reality is an added bonus. The source of true happiness is found within. Access your inner wealth and your outer world will respond.

Conclusion

It's that simple, folks. Relax, Release, Receive, Rhythm and Repeat are the '5 steps to Abundance Activation' and 'Money Manifestation Mastery'. This is the practice of opening up the financial freedom floodgates and connecting deeply to your purpose and the truth of your being. This daily practice helps you to manifest more wealth into your life and keeps you in alignment with your true abundant nature. Ultimately, the purpose of this work is to help you get the most out of your life and your precious time here on this planet.

You have permission to be *wealthy*, permission to be *powerful*, permission to live an *incredible life*. Say 'yes' to your power, say 'yes' to your purpose, say 'yes' to fully showing up. Say 'yes' to living an amazing life, even if others around you are not choosing the same. Say 'yes' to action, 'yes' to collaboration, 'yes' to moving beyond the limitations of your past, 'yes' to experiencing the full potential of your life. Can I get a 'hell yes'?!

One of my greatest challenges in life has been to find the courage to share the truth of who I am. This is why I am so passionate about helping others to live the truth of who they are. I know how difficult it can be.

On my journey, I have been held back by caring what other people think about me. Other people's negative judgements felt like bullets in my chest. To be honest with you, it's still a work in progress. I find myself still being wounded by other people's criticism, but my practice is to stand courageously in my truth, to live a life of joy, pleasure, expansion, freedom and wealth no matter what anyone else thinks.

Being psychically sensitive, an empath, makes this experience intense as I can feel everyone's thoughts, judgements and opinions. These judgements are designed to keep you down, to keep you in your place, to not be too big, too much, too powerful, too great, too happy. And it's incredibly effective! These judgements can hold you back if you buy into them.

I heard once that it won't be the 'powers that be', the 'ruling class', that will control you and keep you small, it will be those we know. It's the subtle and not so subtle messages from our family, friends, community, the media and society that teach us how we are supposed to live and be.

To become a 'Money Manifestation Master', your action is to connect to what is truth for YOU, what is right for YOU and dare to fly beyond the cage that you have been living in no matter what others are choosing around you. Fly free, beautiful being, go and create your wonderful life.

Most people will not choose this level of transformation. Most people will not have the courage to take the action steps necessary to makes their lives better. You are a leader of change on this planet. Change starts with you. Claim it, own it, it's what you are here to be and do.

The most powerful change that you can make on this planet is to become the vibration of joy, freedom, happiness, peace, love and empowerment. Who you *are* in the world has a massive effect on all life around you. You can't always see the impact you have in the world, but you do have one. My inner guidance tells me all the time: *'If you could see the difference you are making by your state of being, you would never doubt or fear.'* Becoming who you are meant to be brings transformational light to all around you.

Nurturing You

There are people in your life that will love you when you step more fully into your power and be inspired when you become wealthier and happier. There are people who will be uplifted and excited by that, and there are people who won't. The brighter your light shines, the more your light reveals the shadow areas that people don't want to feel within themselves. One way for others to stop that uncomfortable feeling is to try to shut your light down. When others judge you, it's not about you, it's about their unwillingness to own what is true about them. They end up projecting their pain onto you to avoid their reality within.

You can't stop people judging you. It's not pleasant to be on the receiving end of judgement. Use the 'Step 2: Releasing' techniques to sweep other people's energy from your system. Hand it back to them with love.

I recommend devoting your time and energy to people and environments that encourage and celebrate you. Choose to spend as little time as possible with those who are not in favour of your light. If you don't have anyone in your life who shares your joy, ask the Universe to bring them to you. They will come.

Go out there and become as powerful, as wealthy, and as joyful as you can possibly be. Follow your heart and soul towards greatness. This is your true nature, this is who you are and why you have come here. You are a gift to the world and all life around you.

I want to thank you for being on this path with me. Thank you for being you, thank you for saying yes to change and sharing your light with the world. It's wonderful to take this journey with you and for us to expand into more, ask for more, and step into the unknown together. You are never alone.

You are infinitely valuable and deeply needed. You have permission to BE. You are safe now. Welcome, dear soul. Thank you for being here.

Remember, you have been birthed onto this planet for growth, expansion and self-discovery with no end point. Make sure to enjoy the ride.